The Light Within

A Soul's Perspective on Life

Lara G. van Oppen

The Light Within

ISBN: 979-8-9947419-0-0   (Paperback)
ISBN: 979-8-9942387-3-8   (Ebook)

Library of Congress Control Number: 2026905451

Cover and interior design by Deborah Perdue, Illumination Graphics

Dedication

For my mother, Els,
whose strength, wisdom, and quiet resilience
continue to guide me, even in her absence.

For Grace,
whose presence, support, and steady love
arrived exactly when it was needed.

For my husband, John,
the calm within my storm,
who holds space for me to come home to,
with unwavering dedication to our family,
and a strength that speaks through action, not words.

For my daughters, Chelsey and Kaitlyn,
may you walk in the footsteps
of the strong women who came before you,
carrying their lessons with you,
and trusting your own inner knowing as you move forward.

Table of Contents

Author's Note

" All will be OK," said the Spirit sitting at the end of my bed, and so my journey into the spiritual realms began. Now, twenty-nine years later, I can honestly say that the Spirit was right, all is OK. Although my life has not been without challenges, in the end, things unfolded in divine timing.

Over the last two decades, I have faced cancer, depression, job losses, the loss of family members, challenges in relationships, hurt, betrayal, and more. Yet, as I sit here writing these words, I realize that just as Spirit told me all those years ago, I am OK.

I imagine that many of you would love to have a similar encounter, to feel reassured that you, too, will be OK. If that is you, please don't give up hope. There is a way to tap into your own personal guidance and inner intelligence, even during the most challenging of times. This book will show you how I navigated the many difficult moments in my life. It will also share guidance and wisdom from beyond the veil. All it asks of you is an open mind.

As you begin reading, I invite you to pause and ask yourself a few questions. Who are you? Who are you really? What shaped you into the person you are today? Are you happy and fulfilled? Do you live a life filled with joy?

These are important questions to ask yourself and they are worth answering. If you can honestly say that you feel content and at peace, that is wonderful. Truly. And yet, I suspect that many of you picking up this book are searching for something more, a deeper meaning, a deeper connection, not only to yourself but also to the spiritual realms. If that resonates with you, then I invite you to continue this journey with me.

The objective of this book is simple and meaningful, to help you become the best version of yourself. This is not only the greatest gift you can give yourself, but also a gift to the world around you. But let's be honest, the journey toward yourself is rarely smooth. It is often filled with obstacles, many of them created by your own fears and conditioning. This path requires patience, tenderness, and a willingness to keep going even when things feel uncomfortable.

When you begin to live in alignment with who you truly are, something shifts. You feel freer, lighter, more at ease within yourself, and without trying, you begin to influence the people around you. When you vibrate at a higher frequency, others feel it. They are drawn to your energy, not because you are trying to lead or teach, but because authenticity naturally invites connection.

We are like waves moving through water, constantly meeting, influencing, and reshaping one another. Every interaction is an energy exchange, and within that exchange lies the opportunity for change. When one person raises their awareness, it creates a ripple effect. From a spiritual perspective, we are all connected, that is to say, what affects one affects the whole. This influence extends beyond what we can see, touching on the greater universe itself. For this reason, it matters deeply what energy we bring into the world.

The chapters in this book will take you on a journey, taking you both inward and beyond what is familiar. Along the way, you will be offered tools and perspectives that allow you the space to uncover who you truly are. Many people are feeling confused and overwhelmed in these times, searching for clarity, direction, and something steady to hold onto. The constant stream of information we are exposed to daily makes it harder to discern what feels true and what does not.

Not just any information, but the information that resonates with your inner knowing and supports your growth.

We are often conditioned to repeat the patterns and choices expected of us by our family, our culture, or our society. Emotionally, many of us are simply doing our best to hold on. Feelings of sadness, anger, anxiety, and depression are all part of this human experience, and I know I am not alone in having felt them. The good news is that many of these emotional states can shift when you are guided toward what is right for you. Yet, it is possible to choose differently, to step onto your own path and create a life that feels true to you. There is no single formula for doing this. We are not meant to be copies of one another. What works for one person may not work for another, and that is exactly as it should be.

You are unique, and you already carry everything you need within you. This uniqueness is waiting patiently to be uncovered. By making small, conscious changes, you can begin to activate your inner guidance system. This will lead you where you need to go, helping you become the person you are meant to be.

It may sound simple, and in many ways, it is, but it also takes courage. Courage to let go of the past, of old identities, and of the person you once believed you had to be Stay strong and stay open, trust the path unfolding before you. This journey, even when it asks much of you, is worth taking. Dive into the unknown and discover who you truly are. You have nothing to lose and everything to gain by taking a chance to become the best version of yourself.

Introduction

By now, you may be curious and wondering who I am, and why I believe I have anything of value to share with you. My answer is simple. I am an ordinary person who has experienced some extraordinary events. It is because of these experiences, and the guidance of several spiritual and celestial beings, that this book came to be. My hope is that by sharing what I have encountered, and the wisdom I have been shown over the years, may also be of benefit to you.

My name is Lara. I was born and raised in the Netherlands, and while growing up, I never imagined that I would one day pack up my life and move halfway across the world. Yet that is exactly what happened. I met my husband in 1987, and after we married in 1989, I said goodbye to my family, my job, and my country. At twenty-one years old, I picked up my entire life, including my two cats, and moved to Southern California. I had no idea what lay ahead of me, but I was ready to embrace the adventure. We settled there and have made it our home ever since.

I have always been sensitive to the energies of others, but the concept for this book came to me in a very specific way. During a guided meditation with my second meditation teacher, Archangel Gabriel appeared before me. At the time, I was still quite new to meditation, yet the experience felt unmistakably real. In Gabriel's presence, I felt illuminated by warmth, love, and light, completely safe and deeply at peace.

While immersed in this gentle and expansive energy, Gabriel handed me a silver pen with a white feather and lovingly conveyed a clear message, to begin writing. At the time, however, I did not follow this guidance. There were several reasons for this. I did not believe I was ready or worthy of sharing my story, as I carried many misconceptions about myself. Life also demanded my attention to raising my family, work, and supporting clients in my Reiki practice, leaving little quiet space to reflect or write.

Although I initially set the message aside, the Universe has a way of gently, and sometimes persistently, guiding us back to what we are meant to do. I continued receiving messages encouraging me to write, and over time they became more frequent and insistent. I host a Reiki circle in my home, and during these gatherings, participants repeatedly shared the same message with me, to start writing. Many of these individuals were complete strangers and had no knowledge of my earlier experience with Archangel Gabriel. Yet the message remained consistent. Eventually, the pull to write became impossible to ignore. I moved beyond my doubts and fears and began to put words to paper.

Even though I completed this book more than eighteen years ago, the words remained dormant, quietly stored on my computer. At the time, I believed I was waiting for the right moment, and looking back now, I understand why. I needed time to heal, to grow, and to move beyond the limiting self-talk that once held me back. Over the past decade, I have navigated many difficult experiences, often by living the principles described within these pages. Because of this, I trust deeply in the guidance shared here, and I believe the time has come for this book to be released into the world. We live in fast-paced and ever-changing times. Many of us feel overwhelmed, pulled in countless directions, and disconnected from our inner knowing. Having tools that help us reconnect with our own insight and power has never been more important. When we operate from a higher perspective, the choices we make not only serve us individually, but also contribute to the greater good.

In the chapters that follow, I will reflect on my experiences and share what I have learned about the nature of the Universe and our connection to it. I will also share spiritual insights and wisdom communicated to me by the Council of Light and other celestial beings. I am not here to convince anyone of anything. I simply share what I have experienced. It is my understanding that we are not alone, and that support is available to us, if we are willing to ask and remain open.

Many people today feel a lack of direction. Beneath this feeling often lies a longing for hope, understanding, acceptance, and unconditional love. On a spiritual level, we are all connected, and learning to understand this connection is essential. Without awareness and responsibility, imbalance persists, with awareness, meaningful change becomes possible.

You are invited to pause, look inward, and consider what you are willing to change. Without self-reflection, lasting change cannot take root, either within us or in the world around us. We are living in unprecedented times, yet these times also hold tremendous opportunity. Old ways of thinking must sometimes fall away to make room for new perspectives to enter our lives. Growth requires space, and space is created when we release what no longer serves us.

This process may feel uncomfortable or even frightening at times. You may feel uncertain or alone. Yet trust that the Universe supports you. New ideas will emerge, new people will appear, and opportunities once closed will open when the time is right. I have lived my life by this guidance repeatedly, and in revisiting these words, I can clearly see how they have shaped who I am today.

My sincere hope is that this book becomes a gentle guide for your own journey. Begin with small, meaningful changes, and allow them to build over time. As you connect more deeply with your inner guidance, you may find there is no desire to return to the way things once were. Moving into the unknown is not something to fear, it is an invitation to expand, to grow, and to discover new possibilities.

Be brave. Take the leap. This is how transformation begins.

Part 1
PERSONAL EXPERIENCES,
AWAKENINGS,
AND INTUITIVE ENCOUNTERS

Beyond Borders

*"To expose yourself to different cultures and viewpoints
is to expand your soul."*

I consider myself very lucky to have been exposed to diverse cultures from an early age. Thanks to my father's work as a Merchant Marine, I was able to travel with him and experience the world firsthand. Moving between places at such a young age quietly shaped my inner world, long before I had words to express them. I believe that exposure to different cultures opens the mind, fosters empathy, and enriches life in countless ways. Even small experiences can expand your heart and perspective.

In this day and age, with all the volatile energies we are experiencing, it feels more important than ever to put ourselves in someone else's shoes. When we stay confined to the mindset of your own cultures, communities, or comfort zones, life can begin to look one dimensional. Opening ourselves to people from all walks of life broadens your spirit, softens your judgment and deepens your compassion.

My father spent nearly thirty-nine years working at sea, transporting cargo across the globe. During our summer vacations, my sister and I sometimes joined him aboard his ship, a unique and remarkable experience that allowed us to see the world at a young age. Those voyages shaped my early view of the world and some of my earliest memories are; At eight, I was driven through New York City by a port agent. By twelve, I had traveled through the Panama Canal, sailing as far as Vancouver and back. At eighteen, I visited Miami and Houston and sailed through the Gulf of Mexico. For a young Dutch girl, these experiences were nothing short of magical.

One memory from New York has stayed with me vividly. We took an elevator to the top of a tall tower, I am not sure whether it was the Empire State Building or the Twin Towers, but I do recall standing there in awe as the cars below looked like tiny matchboxes. When we came back down, I noticed something entirely different, the sharp contrast between wealth and poverty. Sleek black limousines passed by homeless people sitting on the sidewalks. It was the first time I had witnessed such visible inequality, and it left a deep impression on my young mind.

Now living in the U.S., I know that homelessness isn't confined to one city, it's a reflection of a greater imbalance that touches many places. Still, these things remain far less visible in the Netherlands.

The longest voyage I took with my father was when I was twelve years old. It was 1980, and we left during the summer just before I was to start high school. Our trip lasted two and a half months, and I returned three weeks after the school year had already begun.

After spending weeks under the sun in Central American, I came home deeply tanned, so much so that a friend's mother didn't even recognize me when I knocked on her door and sent me on my way. We laughed about it for years.

That particular journey took us from the Netherlands through the Panama Canal and up the coast of Mexico, California, and Oregon, all the way to Vancouver, Canada, and back again. What stood out most to me, and still does, was witnessing people living with so little yet smiling with so much joy. In places like San Salvador, Nicaragua, and Panama, I saw families whose homes were made of a few sheets of metal, yet their faces shone with happiness. Their wealth wasn't in possessions, but in the love and connection that surrounded them. I remember that in Panama, at one of the local markets, the colors, sounds, and smells were overwhelming. Fruits and vegetables were stacked high, and skinned animals hung from hooks. It was raw, real, and entirely different from what I was used to seeing at home. But rather than judging it, I felt awe, a deep appreciation for the many ways life can be lived.

During that same voyage, I threw a message in a bottle into the ocean, with my address tucked inside. Months later, I received a letter from a boy in Florida who had found it. We became pen pals for a while, writing across the Atlantic, a small miracle of connection. Even as a child, I sensed that the world had ways of responding back when you reached out.

I also remember the joy of giving. Once, a port agent and his family visited our ship. His daughters and I played the game *Operation*, and when they left, we gave them the game as a gift. The sparkle in their eyes showed me that joy doesn't need to be grand, it simply needs to be shared. That moment shaped the way I would later treat others: kindness in small acts can have a tremendous impact and the ripple effect can reach much farther than we imagine.

In Nicaragua, a guard carrying a machine gun was assigned to escort us ashore. I later came to understand that this took place during a time of political unrest. As a child, however, I did not grasp the gravity of the situation. I was simply aware that the world could be both beautiful and unpredictable, unaware of the dangers as we walked through the town. Even so, the experience left a lasting impression, one I have never forgotten.

I also learned quickly that as I matured, the way others related to me began to change. I received different messages from both men and women, some welcome and affirming, others deeply unsettling. I attracted the attention of two crew members, one Spanish and another from my country, both attempting to cross boundaries and initiate inappropriate contact. Thankfully, I was able to trust myself, pushed them away, remained firm, and removed myself before anything happened. Later on the journey, I was chased through the ship by yet another crew, one of the officers, running through the loading deck with my heart racing, fully aware of the danger in that moment, I was only twelve after all.

At the same time, I experienced a different kind of tension, quieter but still unsettling, from one of the wives who became fixated on tanning darker than me. It made for some awkward moments on the ship, since I tan very easily; it comes naturally to me. These experiences, though very different in nature, left an imprint. Crossing borders does not only mean moving through new places, it means encountering parts of humanity that challenge our sense of safety, worth, and belonging. I came to understand that if I hold on to fear, discomfort, or resentment, I continue to carry that energy with me. Instead, I choose forgiveness and letting go, not to excuse what happened, but to release myself from its weight and continue forward with clarity and growth.

Later, when I was sixteen, I had a similar awakening on a school trip to East Berlin. This was when the Berlin wall was still in existence. We crossed Checkpoint Charlie and walked across Alexanderplatz, where all the locals stared at us. Our local guide explained that people stared because most of us were wearing jeans. In East Berlin jeans could only be bought on the black market and cost about three months' wages. This experience served as a reminder of how freedom and access, things I took for granted, could be rare luxuries elsewhere. That awareness never left me.

All these experiences gave me more than memories; they shaped the way I see the world. They taught me that happiness is not tied to material things, but to connection, gratitude, and perspective. I saw joy thriving in people who own little, and that truth has guided me ever since.

In Western culture, we are taught that happiness is to accumulate more, bigger homes, better cars, higher status. But happiness doesn't live there. It lives in presence, simplicity, and in the relationships that nourish us. You can't buy that kind of fulfillment. So, where do you begin? Start by asking yourself:

- Am I happy?
- If the answer is no, what will bring me closer to happiness?
- Does my day-to-day life still inspire and challenge me?
- What will it take to feel curious and alive again?
- In a perfect world, what would my life look like?
- If I can't change my surroundings, can I change how I see them?
- Can I take the first small step to incorporate something new into my life?
- Am I willing to let go of what no longer serves me to make room for new things to enter my life?

Take time to assess your life and appreciate the good that already exists. Happiness isn't constant, it's made up of moments that sparkle with truth and connection. Be grateful for the people you love, forgive where you can, and keep growing. Time will pass regardless, so make it meaningful.

At the end of your journey, what remains are not the things you owned, but the love you gave, the memories you created, and the legacy of your presence. Life invites us, again and again, to grow, to remain curious, and to step gently into the unknown, where the next version of ourselves awaits.

Peeling Back the Layers

"The truth was always within me, waiting patiently to be uncovered, layer by layer, until I found my authentic self."

I began my spiritual journey more than thirty years ago, and I remain deeply grateful that I did. What started as a quiet, inward curiosity slowly opened me to new ideas, perspectives, and experiences that shaped me in ways I could not have imagined at the time. That journey gently transformed me from a shy, withdrawn girl into the confident woman I am today. Looking back, I see that true growth never happens all at once. It begins with a single, courageous step, followed by many small moments of willingness and self-honesty.

I have come to believe that this kind of transformation is available to anyone who is willing to turn inward and explore themselves with curiosity and compassion. It does not require perfection or certainty, only the courage to question, to listen, and to begin peeling back the layers, one at a time. This chapter is an invitation to slow down, to look beneath the surface, and to gently notice what has been shaping you, patiently, openly, and without judgment.

Beginning your spiritual journey often feels like being dropped into the middle of a forest with no map. Every path seems promising; every answer lies just out of reach. To make sense of it all, you begin looking outside yourself for guidance, reading books, attending gatherings, and traveling to distant places in search of meaning. We all do this. Despite all the directions I took in search of answers, I eventually realized something important: every path led me back to myself. The truth was always within me, waiting patiently to be uncovered. But to reach it, I had to do the difficult work of going inward and facing my shadows.

This inner work took many years, and at times, the path was difficult, challenging, and isolating. Still, I kept going, peeling back layer after layer until I reached my core. There, I found both the most uncomfortable truths and the greatest freedom. It was in that raw place that I began to step into my authentic self. Looking back, I would do it all over again to be where I am today. Don't be afraid to venture into the unknown. It's essential for your growth.

At the beginning of your spiritual journey, you will likely seek knowledge, guidance, and wisdom from others, just as I did. You'll encounter different perspectives, strong personalities, and like-minded seekers. Fortunately, today's spiritual landscape is diverse and abundant. Whether you devour books or travel to an ashram in India, you can tailor your spiritual path to your own needs. Just remember to be discerning about who you follow and what truths you accept. If something feels off, trust your instinct. If it seems too good to be true, walk away. The quicker you learn to trust your inner compass, the sooner you'll return to yourself.

Eventually, there comes a point where outside guidance no longer satisfies you. Books that once held your interest lose their appeal. Spiritual teachers who once inspired you no longer resonate. This isn't a sign of failure; it's a sign that you're ready for more. Every student must, at some point, move beyond their teacher. To stay too long keeps you co-dependent and risks stunting your spiritual development.

Unfortunately, this transition isn't always smooth. There may be emotional fallout, especially if the bond with a teacher or group was deep. But this separation is necessary. It allows you to step fully into your own power. Often, you've sensed that the connection wasn't serving you anymore, you were just too afraid to let go. For me, this realization came in a dream, where a veil lifted between me and the spirit world. In that dream, I was driving my van when it suddenly began to move backward toward a cliff. No matter how hard I pressed the brakes, I could not stop it. The van kept rolling closer to the edge until it finally went over, and I felt myself falling. In that moment, I saw an image of a veil moving from right to left, and then I woke up. The next morning, everything appeared more vibrant, more colorful, and strangely peaceful. I understood that something within me had shifted, as if I had awakened to a deeper, universal knowing. Even though the van, and I within it, had fallen into the ravine, I felt divinely protected. I suddenly knew there was far more to life than what meets the eye. That moment of clarity marked the beginning of my true independence.

Once you awaken, the path ahead can feel lonely. You may find yourself letting go of relationships with people who can't or won't support your growth. Some may accept the new you, but others will not. While it can feel isolating, something inside you knows there's more. You have an inner drive that pushes you forward, even as outside sources no longer support you. That the turning point when you must begin turning inward, relying on your own strength and your own truth. At that precise moment, you let go and surrender. This is where true awakening begins.

Just like an onion, you are made up of layers. And peeling back those layers is a process. It takes time and care. Move too fast, and the emotions may overwhelm you. Move too slowly, and life may interfere. Worse, you might get stuck in victim mode, where your ego takes over and tries to sabotage your progress. Your mind and ego are in a constant dance, and the ego doesn't like to give up control. If you're inconsistent or unwilling to face the hard truths, the ego will do everything it can to keep you where you are.

This is where many people stall. Some who criticize spirituality or the "New Age movement" are often the ones who never started the real work. It's easier to judge others than to turn inward and examine yourself. But the truth is, no one is perfect. There's always more work to do.

This wisdom isn't meant to stay buried, it's there to guide you. Take time each day to reflect and ask yourself questions. Be aware that painful emotions may rise hurt, anger, fear. These are old defense mechanisms trying to protect you. Acknowledge them, but don't let them control you. Observe them with compassion and ask, *does this still serve me?* If not, let it go. If yes, ask yourself why. Where did it come from? What purpose did it once serve?

Battling your own mind is no easy task. Old patterns will fight to stay alive. But once you release them, you'll uncover the real you. Living from a place of authenticity gives you strength, and others will feel it. They'll begin treating you as you are, not as they think you should be. They'll reflect your light back to you.

If you want to evolve, if you truly want to awaken your soul, you must begin the inner excavation. Yes, it's daunting, but how can you become a new you without releasing the old? Let the process unfold naturally. Don't interfere. Your wisdom is already there, waiting to be uncovered.

That's the power of inner transformation. What a change you can make in the world simply by becoming who you truly are. When you live from your core, the answers you once sought from others begin to rise within you. And with those answers comes clarity, direction, and purpose. It is as if you finally plugged in your inner light and are following your uniqueness to shine.

Be your own detective. Be your own advocate. Discover just how powerful you truly are. Live the life you dream of. And let your light spread to everyone around you. That alone is a service to the world.

Take the first step. Find your spark and share it.

Finding Your Voice

"Let your voice have a positive impact. Don't wait.
You are not serving anybody by keeping your truth.
hidden from the world."

There is nothing more powerful than one's true voice. Our voices carry a unique vibration and holds great power and energy that allow us to speak our truth. But what is our truth? That is a question each of us must explore for ourselves. It is not something we are simply given; it is something we uncover over time, often after years of holding back the words we once wanted to say.

Sadly, even as we move through 2025, many people around the world still live within cultures or religious frameworks that discourage, or even forbid, the expression of personal truth. Even in places where free speech is protected, many struggle to speak freely because of internalized beliefs passed down through families, traditions, and communities. Over time, we learn to repeat what we were taught rather than express what we truly feel or believe.

This challenge is especially prevalent among women. From a young age, many girls are taught to stay quiet, not to rock the boat, and to be seen but not heard. This conditioning can last well into adulthood. In my Reiki practice, I see this firsthand. Many clients, especially women, experience energetic blockages in the throat chakra, often alongside the solar plexus, the stomach area, and the sacral chakra, the area around the belly button. These are common places where emotions are held and suppressed, particularly when speaking or expressing feelings has not felt safe.

This does not mean men are unaffected. Men experience energetic blockages as well, though they often appear differently. Suppressed emotions are frequently stored in the root chakra, which relates to safety, survival, and stability. When emotional expression has been discouraged, these unprocessed feelings may surface as anger, frustration, or irritability. Anger is often one of the few emotions men have been socially allowed to express, making it a familiar outlet for deeper emotions such as fear, sadness, or grief.

Understanding where emotions are held in the body helps us recognize how unexpressed feelings influence our reactions, relationships, and patterns in everyday life. When emotions remain hidden, unacknowledged and unexpressed, they do not simply disappear. Over time, they can manifest as physical illness.

Finding my own voice was a drawn out and difficult process. It required me to dig deep and release a great deal of emotional baggage, but thankfully, I succeeded. I share this as a ray of hope. If I can find my voice, so can you. In the chapters ahead, I will share several reasons why it took me so long. If you are reading these words, you can see that I have found my voice and I am choosing to honor it.

My mother always told me that as a toddler, I was happy, outgoing, and adventurous. Somewhere along the way, that carelessness began to shift as the influence of others slowly diminished my light. This did not happen overnight, but gradually, through moments where my actions were frowned upon, my words were misunderstood, interpreted incorrectly, or simply ignored. I grew up surrounded by strong-minded family members who had no hesitation in speaking their minds but had little patience to truly listen to mine. Like most people, all I wanted was to be heard, accepted, loved, and respected in my own right, not measured against cultural, familial, or societal standards.

When I was very young, around the age of three, my voice was already learning to disappear. After an experience that should never have happened, I tried to express that something was wrong. My words were not met with attention or protection. The adults around me were busy, focused elsewhere, and I was quietly pushed aside. Nothing was spoken about, nothing was acknowledged, and the moment was left unresolved. Without understanding what had occurred, I learned that speaking up did not bring safety. Silence felt easier, and so I adapted. That early experience, unnamed and unspoken for decades, became one of the first places where my voice learned to retreat.

A year later, another experience quietly deepened this pattern when I was four years old. I fell out of my bedroom window and broke my leg, resulting in a two-and-a-half-month stay in the hospital. I lay there with my leg in traction, completely immobile. My world suddenly became very small, a single room with a bed, white walls, a large window facing the hallway, and a rigid daily routine over which I had no control. Each day, I was asked what I wanted to eat. I would answer, only to have my choice dismissed and replaced, often by the same nurse. When I refused the food, I was made to eat anyway. In my small body, unable to move or leave, I felt powerless. I had no words for what I was experiencing, only the deep sense of not being heard.

Something settled inside me during that time. I learned, long before I could name it, that my voice did not carry weight and that resistance only made things harder. Enduring quietly felt safer than protesting. That lesson stayed with me far beyond those hospital walls.

Another memory that deepened this feeling of not being heard surfaced when my bicycle was stolen. I was twelve years old and in high school, and I was devastated. I loved that red bike and pleaded with my mother, trying to explain that I truly did not know what had happened. Once again, I felt unacknowledged and unheard, a familiar experience that had been present since I was a toddler. It felt as though the situation was somehow attributed to me, even though it was completely beyond my control. Eventually, my brother took me to the police station to file a report, but by then the emotional damage was already done. I felt unseen and quietly responsible, despite having done nothing wrong. For months afterward, I rode my father's old bicycle to school. It was heavy, had no gears, and was difficult to manage. In the Netherlands, bicycles are not a luxury, they are your transportation to school, to the next town, and everywhere in between. Each ride echoed an earlier lesson I had learned as a child, that my explanations were often overlooked and that I needed to adapt, endure, and move forward on my own. Looking back, I can see how moments like these shaped my adult tendency to overexplain, to take responsibility for situations beyond my control, and to question whether my voice truly mattered.

Moving between countries and cultures did not help. In fact, it deepened these patterns. Each transition required adaptation, learning another language, understanding new social norms, and living with a constant awareness of being different. Rather than finding my voice, I became quieter and more withdrawn. Silence became my protection, not by conscious choice, but as a learned response. Observing felt easier than participating, listening felt safer than speaking up. I moved further inward, becoming more cautious, slowly trading my natural expressiveness for protective restraint.

This pattern also showed up in my relationships for many years. People often spoke over me rather than with me. Boundaries were crossed because those around me spoke with certainty and force, leaving little room for my thoughts, my timing, or my voice. When I attempted to speak up, I was often overruled and not heard. I can now see the role I played in this dynamic. I could have learned to speak up sooner. However, because of the many experiences I faced, the message I received repeatedly was" you're not good enough", This wasn't just communicated through words but also through energy and silence. From this, I learned that speaking up was not safe. It has taken me this long, well into my fifties, to step out of that shell.

After one of my early experiences with Spirit, my curiosity deepened, and I chose to explore meditation more intentionally. That curiosity eventually led me to take a meditation workshop, which quietly opened the door to a much deeper inner life. While these experiences felt natural and meaningful to me, I kept them largely to myself.

For many years, I learned to separate my inner world from my outer one. Just as I had done in relationships, I kept parts of myself hidden out of fear of being judged or misunderstood. Meditation was often dismissed as "woo-woo," and at times even framed as spiritually unsafe by those who did not understand it. Living and working in a community shaped largely by fundamental Christian beliefs, I did not feel safe speaking openly about my experiences or perspectives. So, I stayed quiet, once again choosing silence as a way to belong.

Learning to speak up and to use my voice was uncomfortable at first. The fear of being misunderstood or causing disappointment often lingered in the back of my mind. Slowly but steadily, with each small step and every moment of successful communication, I began to reclaim the parts of myself that had been silenced long ago. Along the way, I also learned discernment, when to speak and when to remain quiet, when to react and when to pause, when to raise my voice and know when to whisper.

Today, I can look back at the child within that has lived through so many moments and events without a voice. I take care of her now and honor her by respecting myself and my voice. I know that I have something to say, and I am no longer afraid to say it. it. Even now, I sometimes encounter resistance to my words or my presence, but I understand that this is not a reflection of me. I've come to see that if there is resistance, perhaps it reflects the limitations of others. While those moments can still be painful, I am strong enough today to move through them and transform that experience into personal power.

My message to you is this, as I said before, if I can find my voice, so can you. Find your voice despite the challenges you may face, and once you find it, honor it. Begin small but start, take the first step.

Take singing lessons, share your feelings with a trusted friend, or simply speak your truth out loud. Do not wait. You are not serving anyone by keeping your thoughts and emotions hidden. Let your voice have a positive impact, you never know what difference it can make in somebody's life!

Perfect Timing

"Trust that the Universe has your back. Everything unfolds in perfect timing—let that truth settle into your heart and walk your path with peace."

There is a major difference between Universal timing and human timing, and unfortunately for us, that difference can sometimes lead to deep disappointment. As humans, when we're faced with a challenge or desire, we often want immediate results. When things don't unfold on our timeline, impatience sets in. Energetically, however, things move at a much slower pace. That slower pace invites emotional maturity and, most importantly, patience.

I won't pretend it's easy; I've certainly struggled with this myself. But when we accept that the Universe is working on our behalf, according to its own divine schedule and not ours, life becomes a lot more peaceful. If we can step aside and allow things to unfold naturally, we create space to enjoy the process, and sometimes, we even notice the silver linings along the way.

I was blessed to attend several of Wayne Dyer's conferences, and one of his teachings has always stayed with me. He spoke about the concept of "Edging God Out", which forms the acronym for "Ego". He used the example of a woman carrying a child for nine months. During that time, the Universe provides everything needed for the child to grow and develop. But as soon as the baby is born, we humans suddenly take over and assume control, forgetting that nature had it handled all along.

The baby needs time to find its innate rhythm, to bond with its mother, and to begin feeding. Mother's milk designed with all the nutrients the baby needs, yet we often interrupt that natural process. When I was pregnant with my daughters, I used the Bradley Method (natural birth without medicine) and had to advocate for myself during both births. In 1990, I had to push back against hospital staff who wanted to intervene. One doctor wanted me to come in for a scheduled C-section simply because my contractions were not moving quickly enough. Instead, I chose to go home, walk around the block, and return later. My daughter was born naturally the next morning. This experience taught me to keep fighting for what is important and not just conform to existing ideas. It taught me to stand my ground and honor my inner voice.

On a spiritual level, everything works out in perfect timing. If we remain faithful and stay on the course, all will be revealed in time. The challenge is that we want what we want, and we usually want it now. So how do we bridge this gap between human impatience and divine pacing?

There was a time when I believed that staying in control was the only way to feel safe. I carefully planned, anticipated outcomes, and carried a constant sense of responsibility for how things would unfold. Over time, this effort began to weigh on me, and I felt increasingly disconnected from myself. The turning point came when I realized that despite all my effort, I no longer felt whole. I chose to stop forcing a solution and consciously surrendered the situation to the Universe, trusting that clarity would arrive when it was meant to.

The abuse I had suffered at a very young age had weighed heavily on my heart and quietly influenced my life, silencing my voice for decades. One day, I realized I no longer wanted to carry that energy within me. In releasing the need to control how or when this truth should be spoken, the Universe provided the perfect space and timing. I found myself able to share the experience with my mother in a calm, nonjudgmental, and deeply accepting way. What I had feared for so long unfolded with tenderness rather than pain. In that moment, I understood that when we trust divine timing, healing arrives not only when we are ready to speak, but when the listener is ready to hear.

This encourages me to start reconnecting with my spiritual self. I had heard people talk about meditation but never tried it. One day I was pulled to take a class on meditation. My first experiences with meditation were both exciting and, at times, unsettling. Everything felt new, and opening myself inward required a level of trust I had never practiced before. During one of those early moments, I felt a clear and loving connection with my dog Brutus, who had passed on, which reassured me that I was not alone in this unfamiliar space. Shortly after, I became aware of the presence of Archangel Gabriel, whose guidance has since played an instrumental role in helping me find the words and courage to write this book. These experiences did not pull me away from my voice, they helped me recognize it.

Another avenue to pursue is to read spiritual books and access sacred texts such as *"Tao Te Ching"* and *"Change your Thoughts, Change your Life"* by Wayne Dyer. *"The Celestine Prophecies"* also had a great impact and of course the many books I read on Reiki. These practices helped me shift my awareness and remind me that there were other energetic forces to at work beside me in my human body. I was reminded that I am a spiritual being having a physical experience, not the other way around.

If you are feeling impatient about your life not changing or have tried over and over again to make something happen what about taking a pause. Take a breath. Ask yourself: "Is my ego in charge right now? Am I Edging God Out? Am I trying to manufacture something that just isn't in the cards for me? Perhaps if you step back and give the situation some room, things may resolve themselves far better than you imagined. There is a divine lesson in every situation or person.

Trust that the Universe has your back. Know that many souls and beings are encouraging you from the other side. Understand that Universal timing and earthly timing are not the same and adjust accordingly. Have faith that things will show up when you're ready to receive them. Rushing the process only leads to frustration and dissatisfaction. But with patience, you begin to see the world differently.

Everything unfolds in perfect timing. Let that truth settle into your heart and walk your path with peace.

The Gift of Sensitivity

"Your sensitivity is not your weakness, it is your wisdom,
your strength, and your light.
The world needs you exactly as you are."

Being highly sensitive can feel like both a gift and a burden, depending on the moment. The term Highly Sensitive Person is relatively new, yet it is estimated that nearly twenty percent of the population experiences the world this way. Highly sensitive people are deeply aware of their surroundings and more affected emotionally, physically and energetically, by subtle changes in their environment,

Because of this heightened awareness, highly sensitive people often need more time to process and integrate experiences. External stimuli such as loud noises, strong smells, bright lights, or intense emotional environments can feel overwhelming. Common traits include withdrawing when overstimulated, needing alone time to recharge, preferring meaningful one-on-one connections, sensing unspoken emotions in others, and being told they are "too sensitive" or that they feel too much.

Being highly sensitive does not mean you are weak or incapable. Many highly sensitive people pause before speaking or acting, not out of hesitation, but out of depth. This thoughtfulness is often misinterpreted as passivity, when in truth it reflects strong inner awareness and careful discernment.

I have been highly sensitive for as long as I can remember. Loud noises, strong scents, and extreme temperatures affected me deeply from a young age, and I always needed time alone to reset and reflect. For a long time, I resisted this part of myself. I grew up admiring strong women, especially my mother and grandmother, who survived unimaginable hardships during World War II, including years in Japanese prison camps. Compared to their resilience, my sensitivity felt like complete weakness. That belief followed me well into adulthood.

Others reinforced it, often unintentionally. When I cried or withdrew, it was seen as something to overcome rather than something to understand. Over time, I internalized the idea that being sensitive made me less than, even though it was simply how I was wired.

With time and reflection, I came to see sensitivity differently. Because highly sensitive people process experiences deeply and reference past experiences before reacting, they often remain calm in crisis and aware of subtle shifts others might miss. This depth allows for thoughtful responses, even in difficult situations.

I also learned that not everyone experiences emotions with the same intensity. Some people move quickly through conflict or discomfort, while others rely on anger as their primary response. Highly sensitive people tend to carry emotions longer. We feel layers, not just surface reactions. Letting go takes time, compassion, and presence.

For me, unresolved emotional turmoil manifested physically, first through severe pneumonia and later through cancer. While others seemed able to move on, my body held what my mind could not release. I learned that bypassing emotional processing came at a cost. Only by sitting with my feelings, allowing them to move through me, could I begin to heal.

Even now, when I feel unsafe or unseen, my instinct is to withdraw. I close off energetically until I feel grounded again. This is not avoidance, it is self-preservation. Once I feel steady, I can reflect, rationalize, and release. This process has deepened my understanding of both myself and others.

Because emotions are closely tied to memory for me, I remember details vividly. Over time, I learned to embrace both the challenges and gifts of this sensitivity. For example, I still see my mom's face staring down at me from my bedroom window after I had fallen out of it at four years old. I felt the shock and fear when she saw me and that image never left my memory. I am attuned to subtle energy shifts and often sense when something is unspoken or misaligned. One time, I was speaking with a coworker about a matter that required our supervisor's approval. On the surface, she appeared calm and reassuring, telling me that everything would be fine and that it would likely work out. Yet beneath her words, I sensed a current of fear, an unspoken awareness that the request would probably be challenged, if not denied. Holding both her reassurance and her unease at the same time was confusing, and it highlighted how easily I pick up on what is felt but not said. That moment made it clear how my sensitivity often registers emotional truths long before they are openly acknowledged. This awareness is not judgment, but compassion. It allows me to meet others with understanding, even when they are unaware of their own defenses.

If you recognize yourself in these words, know that nothing is wrong with you. You are not broken. You are simply wired differently. Learning to work with your sensitivity rather than against it changes everything.

Sensitivity has also opened the door to intuition. It allows me to connect with universal energy and receive insight that helps guide others on their paths. Through meditation, I began to understand that I could read and sense people's energy, tuning into their bodies and becoming aware of their emotions. During our guided meditation lessons with our teacher, we practiced this regularly, learning how to listen beyond words and trust what we perceived. After I became attuned to Reiki and later formed a Reiki circle with a close friend, this awareness deepened. I noticed that I was not only able to sense energetic blockages and emotional patterns, but that messages of comfort and reassurance would arise simultaneously, offering gentle support to those I was working with. These moments reinforced my trust in my sensitivity and showed me that it could be used in service of healing rather than something to question or suppress. This is not something I take lightly. Sensitivity carries responsibility, to stay grounded, clear, and aligned, to be in alignment with yourself and the Universe in order to receive the messages clearly.

Being highly sensitive does not make you weak or fragile. It makes you aware. With awareness comes the responsibility to rest, reset, and care for yourself. Downtime is not indulgent, it is necessary. Never apologize for honoring your limits.

Grounding practices are essential. Writing, walking in nature, meditation, prayer, meaningful conversation, and humor all help restore balance. Humor, especially, reminds me not to take life too seriously. It does not dismiss pain, but it softens its grip.

The world often encourages us to disconnect from our emotions. Anger becomes easier to express than sadness or vulnerability, yet anger is often a shield protecting unhealed pain. When emotions remain buried, they can manifest as exhaustion, depression, or illness. Healing begins when we are willing to feel and understand what lies beneath the surface.

Honor your sensitivity. Let go of the inner critic that tells you to be different. As you align with your true nature, your energy shifts. Your sensitivity is not your weakness, it calls upon your light, Others will respond to that shift, even if they cannot name it. Some will step closer; others will step away. Allow it. Everyone is on their own journey.

The world needs more sensitivity, not less. Claim it.

In Perfect Alignment

*"Some moments arrive quietly yet carry
the weight of generations."*

After my mom passed away, I stayed in her home for several weeks, the same house I grew up in. Memories echoed through every room, and I became acutely aware of the silence. Once my mom was gone, the house felt different, empty, something essential had shifted.

One Friday, my oldest daughter and I decided to visit Maastricht, a nearby city filled with personal history and meaning. I voiced my concern about parking, since Fridays tend to be busy and hectic, and Maastricht is a popular tourist destination, but we decided to take our chances.

As we approached the city, the sign at our usual parking garage flashed that only fifty-seven spots were left. My stomach tightened, already bracing for the familiar stress of circling the city center in search of a parking space. Yet as soon as we entered the garage, just five spots in, a car was leaving and a space opened up, waiting for us. It felt like a small stroke of luck at the time, though we had no idea it was only the beginning of something much larger.

Once parked, we walked into the heart of the city and made our traditional first stop, the Church of Our Lady, Onze Lieve Vrouwe

Basiliek, to light a candle at the Star of the Sea. These candles are lit as prayers for protection, especially for sailors and for the safe return of those who travel. This ritual has been part of my family for generations; one my daughter and I still honor today.

From there, we headed to our favorite local spot for Belgian fries, and yes, we eat them with mayonnaise. We sat on the steps of City Hall, enjoying the simplicity of the moment. That's when my daughter turned to me and asked if we could go inside. She wanted to see the portrait of my great-grandfather, who served as mayor of Maastricht from 1910 to 1937, his legacy still hanging within those historic walls.

I hesitated, assuming the building would be closed, but we climbed the steps and tried the door anyway. It was locked. Just as we turned to leave, the door opened and a tall man stood before us.

"Can I help you?" he asked.

I explained why we were there and asked if we might take a quick look inside. "Normally not," he said, "but I can show you." We passed a security guard, who gave him a knowing glance, and entered the building.

As we spoke about our family's connection, the man smiled and asked, "Would you like to see the room your great-grandfather worked in?"

"Absolutely," I replied.

We stepped into a room preserved in the elegance of another era, rich with woodwork and history. Then he said something unexpected.

"This is the room I work in."

I paused. "You mean... you're the current mayor of Maastricht?"

"Yes," he said.

I stood there, stunned. We were in the very office where my great-grandfather once led the city, guided by the man who now held the same role. The portrait of my grandfather was still there; our family crest still etched into the stained-glass windows. For a moment, time stood still and everything felt suspended.

We were in the right place at the right time, and we benefited from what the Universe had quietly arranged for us. Some might call this coincidence, but I call it synchronicity, those moments of perfect alignment the Universe offers when we loosen our grip, stay open, and trust that there is more unfolding than we can see. When we do, life meets us in perfect timing.

When we stop forcing outcomes and begin trusting life, something shifts. When we release control and remain open, the Universe orchestrates the most unexpected and beautiful connections. You never know what quiet magic is waiting just a few steps ahead.

Warnings From the Other Side

*"The signs are always there; it's our job to be open and aware.
The other side is watching, guiding, and protecting,
if only we listen."*

I am very aware that we are not alone in the Universe, and that I am able to receive messages from the other side. Even so, the way the Universe communicates never ceases to amaze me. For lack of a better word, "they" are in constant dialogue with me, often through subtle signs woven into ordinary moments.

In the early years of our marriage, my husband traveled frequently for work, sometimes for weeks at a time. During one of his trips to China, something unsettling happened. I was asleep when a loud slamming noise echoed through the upstairs hallway. With only my young daughters and me at home, I became immediately alert. I waited, heard nothing further, and lay back down. Moments later, the sound came again, just as loud.

The second noise felt different. It carried urgency. I got out of bed and checked on my daughters. They were both asleep, but I noticed my youngest was wearing a plastic necklace that did not break easily and could have posed a serious choking risk. I gently removed it. She woke up the next morning safely, unaware of what might have happened.

I believe this was divine intervention, most likely from my maternal grandmother, who was known for being protective and insistent. It felt as though she made sure I did not ignore the warning. That night reinforced my trust in listening when something does not feel right.

A similar story was later shared with me by my sister. While she was away, my brother-in-law was awakened by someone calling his name repeatedly. When he opened his eyes, he saw a spirit standing at the foot of the bed. He immediately checked on my niece, who has a medical condition, and realized she needed urgent care. Once again, a warning had come just in time.

When my sister asked me to tune in, I sensed my niece surrounded by angelic beings. I felt the presence of our maternal grandmother, along with Mother Mary, urgently working to wake her father. Later, we both laughed about how this experience shifted my brother-in-law's perspective. He has always been a very logical, grounded, no-nonsense kind of person, someone who prefers facts over feelings and practical explanations over anything he cannot see or measure. Yet in that moment, logic seemed to soften, giving way to something he could no longer easily dismiss.

If you believe that our essence continues beyond the physical body, then receiving guidance or warnings from the other side does not feel far-fetched. We are supported by guides, loved ones who have crossed over, and other divine beings. With practice and awareness, signs begin to reveal themselves, through song lyrics, a billboard, a bird crossing your path, or a sudden inner knowing.

I have learned to trust my intuition. Guidance often shows up as a sensation in the body, warmth, discomfort, nausea, or a quiet but persistent feeling. Dreams can also carry messages, which is why I keep a notebook nearby at night. Over time, patterns emerge, messages that feel personal and precise.

During a Reiki session with my daughter, I once saw a dark presence standing quietly in the corner of our living room. Rather than fear, I felt recognition. I understood him to be one of my guides and named him Herman, after Herman Munster, since he is tall and dark in presence. He warned me to set energetic boundaries. Minutes later, both my daughter and husband began unloading their stress onto me. Because of that warning, I was able to stay grounded and protect my energy.

Animals have always been messengers for me. A hawk represents my father, a blue jay my paternal grandmother, and a goldfinch my maternal grandmother. Hummingbirds carry the presence of my friend Grace and often signal joy and reassurance.

Once, a hummingbird hovered outside my kitchen window for nearly ten minutes, unfazed by my cat sitting beside me. Another time, one landed nearby while my daughter and I sat in the backyard, singing its song for what felt like an eternity. Both moments carried a sense of calm and safety.

On another occasion, a hawk swooped directly in front of my car as I drove to work. Later that day, I was called into my supervisor's office and questioned about my commitment and work ethic, something completely misaligned with who I am. That morning's hawk had been a warning, and from that moment on, I no longer doubted these signs.

Shortly after we had our house painted, a large grasshopper appeared at our front door. It was unusually big compared to the small ones we normally see where we live. To some, this might seem like coincidence. To me, animals are messengers from God, and grasshoppers symbolize luck and reassurance. It felt like a quiet nod from the Universe, an affirmation that we are supported.

The warnings that night, the awakenings, the birds, the quiet messages, all of them have reaffirmed for me that we are guided and protected. The Universe speaks in many ways. The question is not whether the signs are there, but whether we are willing to listen.

When we learn to quiet the mind and stay aware, we begin to hear the whispers that have been with us all along. In those moments, it becomes clear that we were, and are, never alone.

Universal Sense of Humor

*"Life is the Universe's classroom, every test, every challenge, every
laugh is there to remind you that
growth is the goal, and joy is the reward."*

I am here to tell you that a good sense of humor will take you a
long way. It helps you move through difficulties with more ease
and far less resistance. As we travel through the twists and turns of
life, the Universe has a way of testing us. These moments are not
punishments, but opportunities for growth. Much like finals at the
end of a college semester, the Universe offers its own exams to see
how far we've come. I like to call this the Universal Sense of Humor.

All of us encounter challenges at some point. Most of the time,
we label these experiences as negative, but when we begin to view
them as lessons rather than setbacks, something shifts. You may
have heard the saying, first comes the pebble, then the rock, then
the boulder, and if the lesson is still missed, the mountain appears.
It's the Universe's way of reminding us that learning will happen,
one way or another.

We all have a choice in how we learn our lessons. We can learn
gently, or we can learn through struggle. Paying attention at the pebble stage often saves us from facing the mountain, though sometimes
the mountain is exactly what it takes for true understanding to set
in. For me, this lesson has always been about trust, trust in myself

and trust in the Universe. For years, I doubted my own capabilities and kept myself small, afraid of being seen, judged, or ultimately not loved. That fear quietly guided many of my choices.

The Universe had been gently encouraging me for a long time to begin using my voice in my healing practice, a calling I ignored again and again out of fear and a belief that I was not good enough. I dismissed the signs and messages until one day my throat hurt so intensely that I could no longer ignore what was being asked of me. I opened my mouth and began to sing. The response was immediate. People in my meditation group were deeply moved, and from that moment on, my voice became an integral part of my healing work. Looking back, I recognize that had I continued to ignore the message, the lesson would have returned in a much louder and more painful way. This experience taught me to listen early and make changes at the pebble level, where growth is kinder and the path forward feels far less heavy.

Once a lesson has been presented, the Universe will often revisit it, testing whether it has truly been integrated. That is where its sense of humor reveals itself. The circumstances may change, but the underlying theme remains the same. The first time, it feels overwhelming. The second time, you recognize the pattern. By the third, you might shake your head and think, "Really, again?" Eventually, the lesson no longer carries an emotional charge. You acknowledge it, respond differently, and move on. That's when you know healing has taken place. Even years later, similar test may resurface. Some patterns run deep.

Recently, I found myself in a situation that tested my ability to release the need to be loved or accepted by those who were unable to offer it. This lesson has been part of my life since early childhood and has resurfaced again and again over the past forty years, each time wearing a slightly different face. In the past, I often felt hurt when I did not receive the love, acknowledgment, or simple understanding I longed for from family and friends in Holland. I would change my actions and beliefs to fit what I believed they wanted so I could belong, often at the expense of myself. I carried a quiet ache, believing that if I tried harder or explained better, the connection would finally come.

Over time, I began to understand that my longing was not wrong, but that people can only give what they are capable of giving. My capacity to love is wide and generous, and expecting others to meet me there often left me feeling empty. I once heard a pastor describe people as either pint-sized or ten-gallon-sized in their ability to love. Pint-sized people are not withholding love; they are offering all they have and doing the best they can within their capacity. They are not wrong in their limitation, yet they remain pint-sized in their ability to love. Ten-gallon people are not more right, their capacity to love simply surpasses that of pint-sized people. When these two capacities meet, the difference can leave a quiet but persistent emptiness. When that message truly landed, something shifted. This time, when the familiar pattern appeared, I recognized it quickly and chose to give myself the love I had been seeking elsewhere. In doing so, the lesson lost its power. I stopped looking to others to fill the emptiness and learned to meet myself there instead.

That is often the heart of the teaching. What I had been searching for outside of myself was actually was is usually something I was meant to cultivate within. This realization-built resilience and inner strength in me. I came to the realization that self-reliance does not mean isolation or independence from others, rather, it taught me to no longer rely on someone else to fill a space only I can tend to.

Universal lessons rarely repeat in the same form. They show up through different people, situations, or circumstances, but the emotional trigger feels familiar. If we respond to the trigger, the universe sees that we haven't done the inner work on this lesson. When the reaction is gone, when there is no longer discomfort or charge, the lesson has been integrated. That is when we can naturally let go and move forward.

It helps to remember that we are souls who have human experiences. We are here to expand, evolve, and grow. We do not come to

Earth to suffer, but to learn. Soul growth is not limited to a single lifetime or place. Expansion is ongoing, both for the soul and the Universe itself.

Life becomes much smoother when we stop fighting the process and begin flowing with it. That's why it helps to develop a sense of humor and laugh at ourselves when we can. The Universe certainly has one. I once made the mistake of playfully challenging the Universe. I have a bit of a lead foot when I drive, and I hadn't received a speeding ticket in years. One day, while checking the mail, I joked that I must have finally learned my lesson since it had been so long. Within a week, I received a ticket. Message received. The energy we put out is always met with a response, so it pays to be mindful of what we project. Challenges soften when they are met with curiosity instead of resistance.

Each experience carries an invitation to learn something about ourselves. When we allow change to unfold without fear, we grow simply by participating in the journey. Challenges soften when they are met with curiosity instead of resistance. Developing a sense of humor helps us become students of life rather than a victim of circumstances.

The Universe will keep testing you until you can laugh through the lesson. That's when it knows you've truly learned.

Trust

*"Trust is not the absence of fear; it is the decision to move forward
while listening to your inner knowing."*

At some point in life, all of us are asked to face the question of trust. We may struggle to trust ourselves, find it difficult to trust others because we feel unworthy, or carry wounds from betrayal that make trusting again feel risky or even impossible.

At its core, trust is tied to our most basic human needs, the need to belong, to feel accepted, nurtured, and safe, to have a soft place to land. When these needs are met, trust has room to grow. Slowly, gently, we begin to open again and allow others closer.

If you were fortunate enough to grow up in a nurturing, supportive, and loving environment, trust may have developed naturally for you. But when those elements were missing, trust does not form easily. In those cases, rebuilding trust becomes conscious work, both with yourself and with others. Trust can only exist where there is safety, acceptance, and reciprocity. It is never one-sided. It must flow both ways and be honored over time.

Life has a way of revealing where trust lives and where it does not. Many of us have experienced moments where we believed someone was trustworthy, only to feel deeply disappointed or betrayed. These moments can be devastating. When trust is broken, the pain often cuts far deeper than we expect. The real question becomes, how do we respond?

Betrayal, especially within close or intimate relationships, can leave us feeling hollow, defeated, and wounded. And yet, even here, we are not powerless. We always have a choice. We can cling to the story, replay the hurt, and allow the betrayal to define us. Or we can acknowledge what happened, learn from it, release the painful emotions associated with the event and choose a different way forward.

Many people become trapped in mental replay, reliving the moment over and over. This loop keeps the wound alive and often leads to isolation, depression, and a deepening sense of distrust. But when you choose, and yes, it is a choice, to release the emotional weight, something shifts. Strength returns. Resilience grows. Space opens for healing and new experiences. Trust is reborn.

When trust is broken early in life, especially in childhood, the impact is profound. A child's sense of safety, love, and predictability disappears, leaving confusion about whether people exist to protect or to harm. Children who experience abuse, abandonment, or emotional neglect often internalize the pain. They ask themselves, *"What did I do wrong?"* or *"What is wrong with me?"* Shame and self-doubt take root. But the truth matters here, deeply. The betrayal was never the child's fault. The responsibility belongs solely to the one who crossed the line. Your inner child is innocent.

Healing begins when you stop carrying a burden that was never yours to carry and gently begin to open your heart again.

Choosing to trust, to create your own sense of safety, and to move forward is how you reclaim your life. To do otherwise is to remain stuck in cycles of pain, confusion, anger, and denial. When you stay there, the person who hurt you still holds power over your life. But when you release the grip the past has on you, you step into your own authority. You are no longer defined by what happened. You free yourself to grow, to love, and to trust again.

I know this path intimately. I was abused at a very young age by an extended family member. That experience left a deep imprint, and for many years, I struggled with self-acceptance and trust. Today, at fifty-seven, I can honestly say I am doing well. I have come a long way. Trust will likely always be a tender subject for me, but I live with an open heart. I trust myself, and I trust others. I know now that I am strong enough to face whatever life brings.

The turning point came when I made a decision or decided that the past would no longer define my life. Making that decision was simple. Living it was not. There were moments when I wanted to give up, when the work felt overwhelming. But I stayed. I persevered.

It took me seven years to work through my pain, rebuild my sense of safety, and learn to trust again, especially men. To understand the depth of that journey, know this, at twenty-one, I married my husband and moved from Europe to the United States. That alone required immense trust. I loved him deeply, yet I struggled, not because he gave me reason to doubt him, but because I did not yet trust myself. I feared that if he truly saw all of me, he would not love or accept me. At the time, I did not believe I was worthy.

Now, after almost thirty-six years of marriage, I can say with confidence that we have worked through our differences. I trust him fully. And just as importantly, I trust myself to love and to receive love. Our relationship has grown stronger over time. It has depth, resilience, and truth.

I invite you to open your heart and trust that you are capable of loving and protecting yourself. When you believe in your own strength, you move through the world differently, grounded, resilient, and open, even in the presence of pain or uncertainty. Trust begins within. And when it is rooted there, it allows you to build meaningful, connected relationships, with yourself first, and then with others.

Meditation

I was first introduced to meditation more than twenty-five years ago. After sharing my experience of seeing a spirit with my parents and learning that my grandmother had also experienced visits from the other side, my curiosity about spirituality deepened. I wanted to understand what I had been sensing for most of my life. That curiosity led me to a four-week meditation workshop at our local bookstore. What began as a short course turned into a two-year journey. Our small group of five met every Saturday morning, and those sessions became some of the most transformative experiences of my life.

During one of the early guided meditations, something deeply personal occurred. My dog Brutus, a Malamute mix who had passed away years earlier, appeared to me. From that moment on, he showed up every time I meditated. His presence felt comforting and familiar, a quiet reassurance that I was exactly where I needed to be. Another sign soon followed. Each time I relaxed deeply and felt energy moving through me, I would sneeze. It became a personal marker of connection, a small signal that I was aligned. From this I learned that the Universe often speaks in subtle codes and symbols, if you are willing to notice them.

As I continued meditating, my trust in the process grew. I began to understand that what I had been seeing, sensing, and feeling throughout my life was not imagination, but an essential part of who I am.

Our teacher, Martin, once described me as a radio antenna, constantly picking up information and energy from all directions. That constant openness often left me drained and overwhelmed. I felt anxious, unsure about myself and chronically tired at times due to walking around with other people's energy that I had picked up around me. One of the greatest gifts he gave me was teaching me how to regulate the flow of incoming energy. He showed me how to close myself off energetically by intentionally "locking" my chakras. In my mind's eye, I would turn a key at each energy center, securing it in place before heading into work. This practice created a protective boundary between me and the outside world. Over time, I became so comfortable with it that I learned to choose when to open my energy and when to keep it contained. Learning when to open and when to close changed everything. Instead of being controlled by what came toward me, I learned to choose. That awareness restored my sense of balance and brought with it a deep feeling of freedom.

Several weeks later, during a meditation class led by another teacher, I received two clear messages. The first was an inner knowing that I am a Lightworker. The second appeared as the image of a feathered pen, a quiet yet unmistakable indication that I was meant to write When I later asked the teacher what the term meant, she simply smiled and softly repeated the word back to me. Her gentle response lingered in my mind and stirred a quiet curiosity that led me to seek a deeper understanding, one I eventually discovered through the teachings in *The Lightworker's Way*.

A Lightworker is described as a soul who chooses to live in service to others, offering light and guidance to those who feel lost or overwhelmed. Once I understood this, I made a conscious decision to live in alignment with that calling, to serve where I could and offer light in ways that felt true to me. I will share more about this journey in later chapters.

After two years, our original meditation group disbanded. We studied briefly with another teacher, who eventually acknowledged there was little more she could offer us. Still eager to learn, I reached out to Martin again. For five months, it was just the two of us meeting to meditate in the small back room of the bookstore. That time was meaningful for both of us. He was navigating health challenges, and I was deepening my spiritual practice.

Eventually, Jeanette joined us. She later became a dear friend, my Reiki teacher, and my partner in hosting monthly Reiki circles. It was also during this period that I was introduced to Toning and Sound Healing, something I will explore further in a later chapter.

That modest room at the back of the bookstore played a profound role in my spiritual growth. At the time, resources were limited. There were no online courses, social media, or videos to guide us. Today, meditation and spirituality are widely accepted and openly discussed. This makes meditation much more accessible to everyone. What was once dismissed as unusual is now recognized for its value.

That began to change during the financial crisis of 2008. As uncertainty grew, colleagues started asking how I managed to remain so calm. I cautiously shared parts of my outlook and gently encouraged trust that circumstances would eventually shift. To my surprise, my words were met not with resistance, but with appreciation. Throughout this period, meditation remained my anchor, helping me stay balanced as the work environment became increasingly challenging. It was during this time that I developed a deeper sense of trust and reliance on the Universe. While my coworkers openly shared their beliefs and sometimes judged me for not conforming, the experience, though isolating at times, taught me self-reliance, resilience, and respect for my own path.

Meditation remains one of the most powerful tools I know for inner changes. It opens a doorway to your own wisdom and to something far greater.

To me, meditation is simply defined as spending time in silence with yourself. There is no single right way to do it. You will need to find your own rhythm, your own form of stillness. For me, guided meditation works best, as I am highly visual. For you, it may be something entirely different. Whether through guided meditation, breathwork, walking in nature, or stillness, the most important element is consistency. Even a few quiet moments alone each day can create clarity and calm in ways you might not expect.

My experiences with meditation showed me I was a Lightworker. That awareness brought clarity of purpose that guides me every day. And, while I understood the message I received about writing, I resisted it for many years. Free will allows us to choose our timing. Still, the Universe has a way of gently nudging until we are ready. Over time, Reiki practitioners repeatedly told me, "You need to write." Eventually, the pull became impossible to ignore. I sat down and began. Years later, if you are reading these words, you know that I listened.

At its core, meditation is about being present with yourself. When you grow quiet enough, you begin to tune into your own energy and a deeper intelligence beyond thought. From that place, new perspectives emerge, and life begins to shift naturally. Change does not come from force, but from awareness. When awareness deepens, growth follows, leading us to expand even further in our soul's journey.

Light Worker

*"Your purpose is not to fix everything; your purpose is to shine.
When you stand in your own light, you help others find theirs."*

A Light Worker is often described as someone on a mission, a peaceful warrior whose purpose is to bring light, healing, and guidance to the world. Light Workers choose to come to Earth during times of great transformation to offer support and compassion to humanity.

Today, many Light Workers are incarnated across the planet as we stand at the threshold of a significant shift in human consciousness. Many of you are waking up to the realization that what we are told by our community or nation does no longer hold truth or value for us. We instantly feel that there is more out there than meets the eye, we just don't know where to find the answers. This is where Lightworkers come in. My own understanding of a Light Worker is someone who is simple and grounded. A Light Worker helps another person move beyond their current state of mind, whether on a physical, mental, emotional, or spiritual level. They walk beside others for a time, offering encouragement, tools, and insight, and then they step back. They do not control or direct. They guide, support, and release. In this way, a Light Worker becomes a steady presence during another's dark hour, holding the light until the other person can see it for themselves.

In times like these, Light Workers are needed more than ever. With so many people feeling overwhelmed or disconnected, the role of a Light Worker is to remain grounded, calm, and clear. While it may sometimes feel lonely, this work is never done alone. We are supported by guides, archangels, and loved ones who have crossed over. From a universal perspective, a lifetime passes quickly, like a single breath.

Light Workers help remind others of broader truths; that we are spiritual beings having a temporary human experience, not the other way around and that even when the physical body is left behind, the soul continues. They understand that death is not an ending, but a transition, and that our essence continues. They offer perspective when life feels heavy, showing that what feels overwhelming now will eventually pass. They are here to teach us that life on Earth, with all its contrasts, serves a greater purpose, the expansion of the soul through experience. Without sorrow, joy would have no reference point. This movement between opposites is part of life's design.

When chaos arises, whether personally or collectively, Light Workers are asked to remain steady. They are not here to spread fear, but to radiate calm. During the 2008 financial crisis many of my coworkers felt desperate and lost hope. Through my meditation practice I was given the message that this crisis will turn around and that things would be ok in the long run. I remained calm. So much so that over time, coworkers who had once judged me began to ask questions, and I found myself helping to ease their fears by listening and responding with calm reassurance.

This does not mean they are immune to hardship. In fact, many them experience deep challenges. It is through their own trials that their empathy is born and their wisdom is earned. We cannot guide someone through darkness without having touched it by ourselves. Facing cancer and undergoing treatment increased my trust, faith and patience. It also showed me an internal strength I didn't know was there. Facing the loss of my mom and my best friend forced me to look at life more honestly, to strip away what no longer mattered, and to live with greater intention and presence, to embody the awareness I had spent years cultivating.

Because they are called to support others, self-care is essential for Light Workers. Staying grounded and clear is not optional. It requires awareness of what is taken in, not only food, but information, media, and the energy of those around us. If something consistently drains or destabilizes us, it is worth releasing. Time in nature, meditation, movement, and rest can help restore balance. A calm nervous system and a centered mind naturally hold a higher vibration than one caught in fear or stress.

When storms arise, as they inevitably do, the invitation is to turn inward. It is important for Light Workers to anchor into their connection with Source. This is where our true strength comes from. That is where clarity, calm, and inner knowing reside.

In my own life, I have been supported by other Light Workers who have helped me return to my still point and trust that calm returns after the storm. They have shown me that life moves in cycles, and while we may rise and fall, we are always moving forward. Reiki grounds me through its simple yet powerful principles. These reminders gently bring me back to the present moment and help me choose compassion.

When I later asked the teacher what the term meant, she simply smiled and softly repeated the word back to me. Her gentle response lingered in my mind and stirred a quiet curiosity that led me to seek a deeper understanding, one I eventually discovered through the teachings in *The Lightworker's Way*. A few that continue to guide me are:

Just for today, do not be angry.
Just for today, do not worry.
Just for today, be grateful.
Just for today, work hard and live honestly.
Just for today, be kind to others.
— Mikao Usui

The Tao Te Ching, written by Lao Tzu, also offers guidance through its emphasis on flow, balance, and alignment with the natural order. One passage that has stayed with me reads:

Watch your thoughts, for they become words.
Watch your words, they become actions.
Watch your actions, they become habits.
Watch your habits, they become character.
Watch your character, it becomes your destiny.
— Lao Tzu

As a Light Worker, our role is not to fix everything. It is to shine, to remain present, to offer guidance when asked, and to let go when the time comes. Our light does not need to be forced. It simply needs to be steady. When we stay centered, we naturally illuminate the path for others.

Mindset Changes Everything

*"Mindset changes everything.
Set the tone from the beginning."*

Several years ago, I became seriously ill after a prolonged period of work-related stress. At the time, I was working under a boss who created a toxic and hostile environment. Week after week, the pressure built, until my body could no longer compensate. Eventually, it shut down.

What began as pneumonia quickly became something more serious. Although pneumonia is often manageable with medication, I had a severe allergic reaction to the prescribed antibiotics. My body weakened to the point where I could barely stand or walk. My airways were compromised, and I remained short of breath for months. I spent weeks confined to a bed, unable to return to work. It took nearly six months before I felt like myself again.

As difficult as that time was, it offered me something unexpected, space. Forced stillness gave me the opportunity to reflect on my life and reconsider what truly mattered.

Four years ago, I faced another life-altering moment when I was diagnosed with cancer. Hearing the words "you have cancer" brought everything to a halt. After the initial shock, I made a conscious decision not to surrender to fear. I chose to fight. I underwent four months of chemotherapy and endured the physical and emotional toll that came with it. The process tested me on every level, body, mind, and spirit. I am deeply grateful to have come through it.

Through that experience, one truth became unmistakably clear to me. Cancer is as much a battle of the mind as it is of the body. Where our thoughts rest, whether in fear or in strength, directly affects our ability to heal. I experienced moments of despair and intense physical discomfort, yet I kept returning to the focused decision I had made to live. The human body is remarkably resilient, especially when guided by a strong will and a clear intention to survive.

After the shock of my first chemotherapy treatment wore off, I made a clear decision, I was going to speak up and fight for myself and give myself a voice. First, I talked to my doctor and requested a change to the dosage due to the severity of my side effects. Second, I began by setting small, realistic goals each day. I promised myself I would take a shower daily, and on many days, that was all I had the strength to do. Still, it mattered. It gave me something to hold onto.

When a chemotherapy cycle ended and I entered the short week in between treatments, I began to walk. At first, it was slow and cautious, as I tested the limits of my body. Each day, I went a little farther. By the end of the week, I was able to walk the length of the flood channel in my neighborhood, even though I knew another round of chemotherapy would begin the very next day.

I refused to give in to the negative thoughts that crept in. I made myself eat and drink, even when I had no appetite, and I kept pushing back against fear and exhaustion. This was not about forcing positivity, it was about choosing to keep going. That mindset carried me through, and looking back now, I believe it played a crucial role in my survival.

I also relied heavily on Reiki during my treatments, especially the principle *"just for today, do not worry."* The foundation of Reiki philosophy is held within its original ideals, and throughout my chemotherapy, I leaned on these simple yet powerful reminders to help me stay grounded and present. Rather than thinking far ahead or becoming overwhelmed by uncertainty, I returned again and again to the moment I was in. These principles offered steadiness when my body felt weak and my mind wanted to wander toward fear.

The original Reiki principles are often described as the secret art of inviting happiness and a gentle medicine for all of life's challenges:

Just for today, do not be angry
Just for today, do not worry.
Just for today, be filled with gratitude.
Just for today, devote yourself to your work.
Just for today, be kind to others.
—Mikao Usui

I still work at the same place today, though in a different capacity, and I now use my voice when something does not feel just, whether for myself or for others. I have learned that there is wisdom in silence, and that there are also moments when speaking up is necessary, calmly and with confidence. My mindset has shifted toward looking for the good in each situation and doing what I can to create a positive work environment, not only for myself, but for my coworkers as well.

In small ways, I try to contribute to that atmosphere. I organize monthly birthday celebrations, and I keep a bowl of candy out for anyone who needs a quick lift during the day. This mindset is not always easy to maintain, and some days require more effort than others. Still, I show up and do my best, and I have learned that these small, intentional choices not only strengthen me, but also quietly shape the tone of the day for everyone involved.

You, too, have the opportunity to set the tone for your day. Small, intentional choices, a kind word, a moment of patience, or a simple act of care, can shift how a day unfolds. While we cannot control everything that comes our way, we can influence how we meet it. Over time, these choices shape not only our outlook, but the way we feel at the end of the day, more grounded, more present, and more at ease with ourselves.

This is your power, the ability to set the tone within your own mind and, through that choice, quietly influence change not only within yourself, but in the world around you.

My Introduction to Reiki

"Reiki is not something you do; it's something you allow. When you open yourself to the flow of Universal Life Energy, you open yourself to the infinite possibilities of healing."

During my early twenties, I experienced a wide range of physical symptoms and sought answers from my doctor. I was prescribed several medications, but unfortunately, I had allergic reactions to each one. Some were mild, while others were more severe and took considerable time to recover from. One example was a beta blocker. I was started on a low dose of 10 mg, with the plan to gradually increase to 100 mg daily. After just one dose, I went to bed and began hallucinating, seeing my husband three miles away even though he was lying right next to me. When I reported this to my doctor the next day, he dismissed it as a placebo effect.

After trying other treatments with no effect, several doctors told me they couldn't find anything wrong and made me feel as though my symptoms were all in my head. I felt awful, isolated, and depressed, with nowhere to turn. That's when I decided to take control of my own health. That was 31 years ago, and I've never looked back.

My first step was visiting a homeopathic doctor. After doing my research, I found a licensed and reputable practitioner who spent over an hour listening to my concerns. His conclusion was that my hormones were completely out of balance, which was not surprising after giving birth to two daughters just 11 months and 20 days apart, breastfeeding, and suffering a miscarriage. He treated me with homeopathic drops and adjusted my diet. Within two weeks, I felt 70% better. After 30 days, I felt like a new person.

Looking back, I shouldn't have been surprised that homeopathic medicine worked better for me. As a child, I suffered terribly from seasonal allergies. My hometown in the agricultural region of the Netherlands was surrounded by blooming fields during spring and summer, triggering intense reactions. Our primary doctor gave me allergy shots, but they had no effect. On the advice of my aunt, my mom began taking me to a homeopathic store 40 minutes away. The drops they provided made a noticeable difference. Even after moving to the United States, I continued visiting the store during trips to Holland to restock, until one day, I realized I no longer needed them. Somehow, after living in California for two decades, my allergies had subsided. Let me be clear: I don't believe Western medicine is bad or that doctors aren't helpful. They certainly have their time and place. When I was diagnosed with cancer and underwent chemotherapy, I relied on the experience and guidance of my oncologist. And obviously, a homeopath won't fix a broken bone or perform surgery. That said, I believe holistic and natural medicine are often better suited for treating chronic conditions. Western medicine tends to treat symptoms, while homeopathy seeks to address the root cause. Personally, I've found alternative medicine far more effective, and if Western medicine hasn't worked for you, I encourage you to explore holistic options.

As mentioned in earlier chapters, I began meditating in the back room of our local New Age bookstore. That's where I met Jeanette, a Reiki Master. We became friends, and I decided to take a class on Reiki, becoming attuned to Reiki Level I. After my attunement, life pulled me in other directions, and raising my daughters took priority. A few years later, I returned to Reiki with renewed passion. Within two years, I became a Usui Reiki Master/Teacher and a Karuna

Reiki Master/Teacher. Since then, I've been practicing and teaching Reiki regularly. Jeanette and I co-founded a community Reiki circle. Although she eventually stepped away due to family obligations, I've continued hosting the circle in my home for over 20 years. Through Reiki, I've had the privilege of helping people from all walks of life work through emotional and physical blockages and deepen their spiritual awareness. It has also helped me become my best self.

Reiki is an ancient healing modality based on the teachings of Dr. Mikao Usui. Though its roots trace back to Tibet thousands of years ago, Dr. Usui rediscovered its principles during a 21-day fast on Mt. Kurama in Japan. After traveling through China, India, and the U.S., he returned to Japan, where he undertook a spiritual fast and received the symbols and knowledge we now associate with Reiki.

The word *Reiki* (pronounced "Ray Key") means "Universal Life Energy." It combines two Japanese words: "Rei," meaning universal life, and "Ki," meaning energy. Reiki is a gentle yet powerful form of energy healing that involves the laying on of hands to balance a peron's energy centers (chakras), encouraging the release of physical, emotional, and spiritual blockages.

As a Reiki practitioner, I act as a conduit, allowing healing energy to flow where it is most needed. During a typical Reiki session, I scan the body for energetic blockages, beginning at the head and slowly working my way down to the feet. As I move through each area, I sense and release tension while gently supporting the body with renewed, balanced energy. I often describe a Reiki session as feeling similar to a deep tissue massage, except that I do not physically touch the body. The experience works on an energetic level, allowing tension to release and balance to return in a gentle yet profound way. Reiki enhances vitality, reduces stress, and supports the body's natural healing process. When people ask how Reiki works, I explain that it helps balance the body's energy centers by releasing energy that feels stuck or tense. During my own cancer treatments, I used Reiki to support myself, allowing renewed energy to strengthen my weakened physical body. I would intentionally tune into the Universe and gently draw that energy down through the top of my head, visualizing it filling every cell with white light.

Many of my clients report an immediate sense of release during or after a session, often describing deep calm and relaxation. One client experienced noticeable relief in her lower back by the time the session was complete, while another shared that she felt a profound sense of peace following a session after the loss of a beloved pet. These experiences continue to affirm for me the quiet yet powerful way Reiki supports both the body and the heart.

It can be practiced alongside any medical or spiritual tradition.

Getting to know myself through Reiki has been a profound gift. It has helped me confront deeply buried trauma and has given me the courage to find my voice, ultimately helping me write this book. Understanding that the Universe supports each of us in healing has transformed my perspective and proved invaluable to my mental and emotional well-being. For those curious about Reiki, you can visit my website at www.healingtouchenergies.com.

If you are facing illness or chronic conditions and traditional medicine has not been effective, I encourage you to explore holistic and alternative modes of healing. There is no single path to self-discovery, but Reiki can be a powerful ally. Don't be afraid to open up and begin. It just might change your life.

First Contact

*"When you open to the higher realms, you remember the truth
your soul never forgot."*

Here is where I'm going to ask you to keep an open mind. Trust me, this experience came as much of a surprise to me as it might to you, but let's just say it completely changed my awareness of the Universe.

First things first: we are not alone in the Universe. There, I said it.

I had heard stories about extraterrestrials from spiritual mentors before, but I hadn't taken them seriously, until everything changed. Like many of us, I was familiar with Roswell, New Mexico, and the accounts of unexplained UFO sightings. More recently, the U.S. Navy has even gone public with videos confirming these sightings during training missions. Still, nothing prepared me to actually be in the presence of these outer earthly beings.

As I shared earlier in this book, my first experience with a spirit happened at age twenty-seven, my first contact with extraterrestrial beings came several years later, during a Breathwork workshop I attended with friends. Breathwork is a meditative technique that uses focused breathing, movement, and short periods of rest.

Near the end of the fifth breathing cycle, I felt an energetic pull and release to what I can only describe as yards of black ribbon with a purple tint being pulled from my lower stomach region. Immediately,

I understood this to be years of stored emotional trauma releasing from my body. The emotions connected to this release were intense, and I couldn't stop crying. Then, three tall, white, illuminated beings appeared before me, showering me with warmth, love, and kindness. I felt completely taken by surprise, yet at the same time, the experience was peaceful and beautiful.

The second time I encountered these beings was during another Breathwork session. This time, I felt my energy rise as I was energetically taken into space. The same three beings appeared, guiding me gently onto what I now know was their ship. This ship was white, translucent and just outside of our atmosphere. It was pulsing with energy The walls didn't seem solid; they felt like energy fields. Inside the ship, other similar-looking beings welcomed me. Their bodies were also translucent, with colorful auras radiating from within.

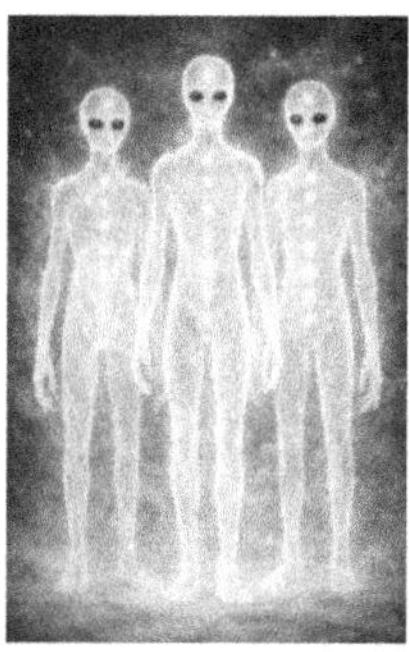

During my time with them, they "showed" me the planet they originated from. It was several star systems away, red, windy, dusty, and surrounded by three moons. Although we did not physically visit their planet, they shared it with me telepathically. In fact, all communication between myself and these beings took place that way. It felt as though a thought was formed and then gently passed to me. On my end, it arrived as a sudden idea or an unexpected knowing, as if new understanding had quietly surfaced in my mind.

While it was hard to wrap my head around what was happening, nothing felt threatening. These beings were kind and respectful, even bowing as I passed by. At first, it made me uncomfortable, as I didn't feel I deserved such reverence. Over time, I came to understand this gesture as a cultural form of acknowledgment, much like we see in certain traditions here on Earth. So, there I was among these ancient beings, looking around their luminous rooms, feeling unexpectedly at home. I wasn't there for long, but to this day, I remember every single moment.

Since that first contact, I've had multiple encounters with these beings, whom I now call the Guardians of the Light. From what I understand, they have watched over humanity for millennia and are here to help guide us through our evolution.

The Guardians of the Light see our lives from a higher perspective. While we perceive tragedy or loss as terrible, they see life on Earth as but a blink of an eye in the grand journey of the soul. To them, death is not an end but a transition, a continuation of growth. Even when we make that transition, they surround us with love and understanding. These celestial beings made me aware that they have been with us for a very long time and will remain long after our own lives have ended, watching over the next generation. The lessons we learn along the way are what stay with us, in this lifetime and the next. Every soul, every lifetime, contributes to the expansion of consciousness.

How can this be, you ask? Why can't everyone see them or be aware of them? Extraterrestrials are not even real, or are they? Imagine a parent watching a toddler learn to walk. The parents lovingly stand by, allowing the child to wobble and fall, encouraging them to rise again and again, while making sure they don't get seriously hurt. These beings do much the same for us.

These Guardians of the Light are present to observe and protect us in their own way. We live on a planet of duality, yin and yang, light and dark, love and fear. Within this duality, growth is possible only through experience. The Guardians are able to intervene energetically, yet much like a parent watching a toddler learn to walk, they allow us to fall a few times before stepping in. Even then, their intervention is subtle and universal rather than personal or forceful.

They have committed themselves to watching over us and supporting our evolution, guiding us as we learn to navigate life beyond the limitations of the ego mind. In many ways, they resemble guardian angels, not here to remove every obstacle, but to help us grow strong enough to move through them. Their purpose is not to shield us from all hardship, but to see us succeed in overcoming fear, conditioning, and self-imposed limitations, so we can live our lives more fully and consciously.

You may wonder why suffering exists if such guidance is available. Why are there wars? Why does conflict repeat itself, both personally and collectively? Much of this pain arises from the ego and its relentless need to be right, to control, or to win. When fear, negativity, or aggression surface, the ego reacts quickly. It seeks retaliation, justification, or dominance rather than understanding. In these moments, we allow fear to lead us, acting from scarcity and separation instead of connection and compassion.

The Guardians remind us that choice is always present. When we slow down, breathe, and choose love instead of fear, something softens, and our response begins to change. We may stumble at times, but we still hold the power to choose awareness, to either fuel the problem or help create the solution.

Ask yourself how often you have been caught in worry or fear, only to later realize that everything turned out fine. That familiar, anxious voice is the ego speaking. On a larger scale, wars emerge from the same patterns, disputes over land, beliefs, power, and identity, all expressions of an unchecked ego. The ego thrives on drama. It creates noise and conflict to distract us from what is truly happening within our emotional, mental, or physical bodies.

This dynamic does not play out only within individuals, but within humanity as a whole. Simply turn on the news and you can see it reflected back to us. What we fail to address within ourselves eventually manifests in the collective. And yet, even within this, guidance remains present, patiently inviting us to choose awareness over reaction, love over fear, and growth over control.

One of the most powerful encounters I had with these beings took place during another visit, when they showed me Earth from the bridge of their ship. I saw dozens of spacecraft stationed nearby, held in perfect alignment. In that moment, the message was unmistakable. Earth is not isolated. We are part of a much larger network of life, and our choices matter. The way we live, think, and respond, especially whether we choose love or fear, sends ripples far beyond our planet. Our collective energy does not stop at Earth's boundaries; when we act from fear, division, or harm, those choices carry weight and create powerful disturbances that impact the wider Universe and the many forms of life connected to it.

On another occasion, I was taken onward to what I have come to think of as the larger ship, the one I often refer to as the Mother Ship. Inside, I was brought into a vast, amphitheater-like hall and gently lowered into its center, where I met the Council of Light. They appeared as twelve equally dressed, wise, and deeply spiritual beings who shared messages meant to be passed on to others. This council is part of what I understand as the Galactic Federation of Light, and they hold a central role within it. For many years, I was not shown their faces, only their robes. More recently, however, I have been allowed to perceive them more clearly. Their faces appear pale, almost stone-like, with strong, angular features, hollow yet wise eyes, and a pointed nose with two small openings. They look remarkably similar to one another.

On other occasions, I have encountered different beings, some resembling praying mantises, immense in stature, as well as what are often referred to as greys, both small and tall. With one exception, these encounters have all felt loving, safe, and deeply enlightening. There was one experience that felt unsettling at first. Two beings appeared and began scanning my energy, as if assessing my spiritual development. Rather than reacting with fear, I recognized what was happening. Years of working with energy had taught me how to stay grounded and centered, and I trusted that knowing.

Before this encounter, I had experienced a powerful dream in which my father was being pulled backward into an energetic field. Instinctively, I drew energy up from my core and projected it outward, breaking the pull and releasing him. In that moment, I understood that focused intention and grounded energy could interrupt forces that did not belong. When the two beings appeared, I applied that same inner knowing. I anchored myself, drew energy from my center, and projected it outward with clarity and intention. The interaction ended immediately, and they were gone. No harm came to me. The experience reinforced my understanding that familiarity with energy, combined with calm presence, allows discernment rather than fear to guide the response. Most encounters, luckily, leave me feeling blessed, expanded, and entrusted with a deeper understanding.

When you connect with the higher realms, you don't gain something new, you remember what your soul has always known. These encounters gently peel back layers of fear, conditioning, and doubt, revealing the truth beneath them. You begin to remember that you are a spiritual being having a human experience, a reflection of Source expressed here on Earth. They do not change who you are, they simply remind you of who you have always been. Through this remembering, you move through life with greater clarity, trust, and compassion, guided not by fear, but by an inner knowing that has quietly lived within you all along.

High Council of Light

"Even the smallest act of kindness ripples across the Universe,
touching more hearts than we can ever imagine."

As I mentioned before, I was introduced to the High Council of Light. This Council consists of twelve celestial beings who, from what I understand, represent the Galactic Federation. These members have been around for millennia, observing us and working to ensure our success as a race. When I visit the High Council, they always invite me to step forward and be in their presence. During most visits, they share a personal message with me. One message affirmed my role as a Lightworker, that I am here to bring change through awareness and presence. Another gently pointed out that I had been holding back, urging me to recommit myself to the work I came here to do. They showed me that my energy was very low and they "filled" me back up, recharging my body ready for action. It was an invitation to step more fully into my purpose and align my actions with my soul's intent. Their kindness and wisdom have been immeasurable and have deeply enriched my life. When they address me, it's always in a peaceful and loving manner, although they can be quite firm at times, keeping me on task and gently reminding me not to slack off.

During my last visit, I was shown an image of Gandhi. Gandhi, in human form, was not a physically imposing man, yet his impact on the world was profound. The message they conveyed was clear: one person can make a massive difference. It all starts with one step, then another. This reminded me that when your intentions are rooted in goodness, your influence can ripple outward and foster positive change. At first, this message felt overwhelming. How could I possibly affect the vast challenges in the world? But the realization came that daily kindness, the way we treat others in small moments, can create the greatest impact. A smile, a kind word, or a simple thank-you can spark a chain reaction of goodwill. That energy travels farther than we know.

You might wonder why they don't do more, why they don't simply intervene. The High Council is aware of the struggles we face on Earth, yet they operate within the Universal Law of Non-Interference. This does not mean they stand by passively. Their support comes in subtler ways, through gentle energetic shifts and by raising the vibration around our planet to encourage positive change.

You may sense their presence as a sudden calm, a quiet inner knowing, or a moment of clarity that feels different from your usual thoughts. It might arrive as a soft nudge toward patience, compassion, or understanding. When you truly feel this shift, it often feels like coming home. There is warmth, serenity, and a deep, familiar peace. In that moment, separation dissolves, and you remember that you are one with the Universe.

These moments are easy to miss if you are moving too fast or caught in fear, which is why stillness matters. When you pause, breathe, and respond from love rather than reaction, your energy begins to meet theirs. In this alignment, you step into your highest version of yourself. From this place, guidance becomes accessible, wisdom flows more clearly, and choices feel grounded rather than forced. What once felt confusing begins to make sense, not because life has changed, but because you have.

This meeting point is where support becomes tangible. Growth unfolds naturally. And you begin to remember the truth your soul has always known. Once you connect with the higher realms, something within you stirs, a quiet remembering. You recognize that you are more than you have been led to believe. You are powerful and eternal, a reflection of Source itself, living a human experience on this planet. You are part of a vast Universe, home to far more wisdom, love, and possibility than the mind can grasp. And as you peel back the layers and return inward, you don't become something new, you simply remember who you have always been.

We live in a world where negativity is amplified, and our conditioning often leads us to dwell on fear or judgment. For instance, you might not speak up or stand up for yourself due to fear of judgements or worse retaliation. But we can choose to disrupt that pattern. We can choose to stand up and speak up, lovingly and with commitment towards ourselves. Each of us can act as a transmuter, an alchemist, turning negative energy into light. That's the true meaning of alchemy, not turning lead into gold, but transforming fear into hope and pain into purpose. Sometimes we don't even realize the influence we have on others. We don't always know what someone is going through, and a small gesture can completely shift their day. You can give someone a compliment, a simple smile or a hug. Most people simply want to be seen, heard, and acknowledged. Offering your time, your presence, or your kindness can be transformative. We are needed now more than ever to hold space for each other and be intentional in our energy. I consciously soften my energy to meet others where they are, gently matching their vibration rather than overpowering it. I might begin with a smile, share a light moment or a simple joke, and allow my body to settle into a more open, positive state. In doing so, the person in front of me feels seen and acknowledged. This small, intentional shift is a simple yet powerful way to change the energy of any interaction.

As the Universe responds to what we put out, you'll notice energetic shifts when you change your energy. I've seen this firsthand. Over the last several months, I've noticed that I am often removed from negative interactions. One day at work, I stepped away to speak with a student and the librarian, only to return and find that a heated confrontation had taken place while I was gone. It was as though I had been shielded. On another occasion, I had stepped away briefly, and when I returned, the energy had noticeably shifted. A coworker had just dealt with an angry parent who had already left by the time I came back. Once again, I found myself protected, untouched by the negativity that had passed through the space.

Of course, I won't always be spared from negativity, but I do believe the frequency I'm putting out is making a difference. We can't control how others behave, but we can control how you respond. If you want to see a better world, commit to being part of that change. Ask yourself each day, *"Did I leave this place better than I found it?"* If the answer is yes, then you can be proud. The Universe and all its inhabitants are grateful for your efforts.

If you want to see love, be love. If you want to feel joy, radiate joy. If you want to eliminate negativity, step away from drama and choose a new perspective. Miracles begin with a shift in energy. Be the light in the dark, shine brightly. That is all these beings ask of us, and I don't believe it is too much to ask. Start today by making a difference. It doesn't have to be big. Start small. In time, the shift will begin to unfold around you.

The Power of Perception

*"Healing begins the moment we choose to see differently. Even a
small shift in perception can open a doorway to peace."*

In my private practice, I am often reminded of how deeply perception shapes our experiences. We tend to see the world through the lens of our beliefs rather than as it truly is. Two people can share the same moment and walk away with entirely different impressions, shaped less by what occurred and more by the meaning each person assigned to it. When those meanings are reinforced over time, they can begin to feel fixed and unquestionable.

What we respond to emotionally is rarely the event itself, but the interpretation we carry forward. As these interpretations become woven into memory, moments in the present can echo the past, causing old emotions to surface as if the original experience is happening again. This is often where trauma takes root, not in the event itself, but in the meaning that continues to live within us.

During Reiki sessions, I often sense energetic blockages connected to unresolved emotional experiences. More often than not, these blockages are not tied to what happened, but to how the experience was perceived and internalized. When perceptions harden, they can interrupt forward movement and lead to patterns such as overthinking, depression, addictive behaviors, or even physical illness.

When someone is caught in this state, it can be difficult to recognize that the past event is no longer the issue. When the ego feels threatened, the body often responds with fight-or flight. Defensiveness rises, and the nervous system stays on high alert.

It is not the event itself that creates suffering, but the meaning attached to it. If someone were to insult you in a language you do not understand, the words would hold no emotional charge. It is only when meaning is assigned that pain arises. This understanding alone has the power to shift how we respond to the world.

In my work, I often witness how deeply perception shapes emotional responses long after an event has passed. When early experiences remain unresolved, their meaning is carried forward and quietly influences present relationships. For instance, someone who grew up without consistent affection may enter adulthood longing for connection, expecting a partner or children to meet a need that was never fulfilled. When love is expressed differently than anticipated, they may feel rejected or unloved, not because love is absent, but because their perception makes it difficult to receive it. Similarly, individuals who have experienced abuse often internalize the belief that something is wrong with them or that they were somehow responsible for what happened. This meaning can become so deeply embedded that it shapes behavior, self-worth, and emotional response for years. The ego, having learned to protect, holds tightly to these interpretations, making them feel fixed and difficult to change. With awareness and support, however, these perceptions can begin to soften, allowing space for healing and a new understanding to emerge.

I have learned that steady, compassionate communication can soften these defenses. Change rarely happens all at once, but when a seed is planted with care, it has the potential to grow. Faith plays a role here, trusting that once awareness begins, the Universe supports the process of integration. Shifting one's perception takes time and requires a safe, non-judgmental environment. Safety is essential. Only when someone feels secure can they begin to explore new perspectives. From there, I gently invite them to consider alternative ways of seeing their experience. It is often not the abuse, or the person involved, that creates lasting pain, but the meaning we continue to assign to the experience and the thoughts that return to it again and again, causing lasting damage to our well-being. This process can feel uncomfortable, as the ego naturally resists change. Its role is protection, yet sometimes it protects us so fiercely that it keeps us anchored to beliefs that no longer serve us.

Wayne Dyer captured this beautifully when he said, "When you change the way you look at things, the things you look at change." I have seen this play out repeatedly. Healing often begins the moment a small opening appears, just enough space for a new interpretation to take root.

Projection is closely connected to perception. It occurs when we assume others see or feel the same way we do. This often leads to disappointment when reality does not align with expectation. After my mother passed away last year, I was devastated. For nearly a year, I woke each morning with a constant ache around my heart. I missed her so deeply that I often wondered how I would make it through each day. In my grief, I projected my pain onto others, expecting them to feel what I felt, only to discover that this was not their experience. Some spoke of relief and a sense of freedom, which left me feeling even more alone in my grief. Each person views the world through their own lens. While we cannot control others, we can choose how we respond.

Changing long-held patterns takes time. Be patient with yourself. Notice progress, even when it feels small. Growth is rarely linear, and the journey itself is part of the transformation. With awareness and compassion, perception softens, and with that shift, new possibilities emerge.

When Hurt Rises to the Surface

"Hurt rises not to break you, but to show you where you have outgrown what once defined you."

There are moments in life when old hurt rises within new situations. Not because the pain has returned, but because you are finally ready to see the experience from a different perspective. These moments often arrive without warning and touch the places that still long for belonging, acceptance, and understanding.

For me, this has been a recurring lesson for more than fifty years. The Universe has a way of bringing these moments forward until we are ready to release what they came to teach us. Recently, another such moment found me. It emerged unexpectedly through a conversation with my family, leaving me once again feeling unseen and misunderstood. This came about not because anyone intended harm, but because we do not experience or interpret the world in the same Their words brushed up against an old wound, one rooted in beliefs I had carried for much of my life, beliefs I was taught, both subtly and directly, to accept as truth. Their comments shone a light on familiar emotions, the feeling that I was different, difficult to understand, or somehow not enough.

Growing up, my sensitivity made me acutely aware of my surroundings. I moved through life guided by intuition and emotion, sensing what others might overlook and feeling what often remained unspoken. Experiencing the world through my heart felt natural to me.

My family, however, moves differently. They ground themselves in structure and practicality. They think before they feel and often keep emotion at a comfortable distance. I move inward while they move outward. I seek closeness; they value neutrality. I enter experiences directly, while they step back to assess. Though bound by love, our inner worlds are built differently.

For many years, I hoped we could meet somewhere in the middle. I tried to understand their way of being and waited for a moment when they might understand mine. I adapted, softened, and made myself smaller, not because I wanted to disappear, but because I wanted to belong. I longed for a space where connection felt mutual, where I did not have to explain myself to be understood.

I used humor, helpfulness, and flexibility to bridge the distance. Still, I often felt reached for only when something was needed, not because of who I am emotionally. Perhaps this is one reason I married outside my culture and eventually moved across the world, seeking environments where connection, openness, and emotional exchange felt more natural.

Living between two cultures added another layer to me feeling inadequate and different. I have lived in the United States for over thirty-seven years. I am no longer fully Dutch, even though I try each time I return. My language has shifted, my expressions have changed, and my thinking has been shaped by a different emotional culture. While I still make an effort to preserve my roots, this is not always seen or acknowledged. In the eyes of my family of origin, precision and correctness matter deeply, and I often fall outside those lines. I am simply not the same person I once was.

Recently, this difference became visible again during a phone call with a family member. It became clear once again that my family communicates through logic and fact, I communicate through feeling and presence. They feel safe in distance, while I feel safe in closeness. In that gap, the familiar ache to connect with them resurfaced. Emotional reciprocity matters deeply to me, and it always has.

The hurt appeared first in my body. My chest tightened, my shoulders tensed, and a heaviness settled around my heart. Old emotions often ask to be felt before they can be released, so I stayed with the sensation, breathing through it rather than pushing it away. Slowly, clarity began to emerge. I realized I was not hurting because of what had been said. I was hurting because I was finally facing a truth I had resisted for a long time. I had lost two people who deeply understood, accepted, and loved me. The people I had hoped would step into that space may never fully be able to, not because they do not love me, but because they love in a different way. Not because I am wrong, but because I am wired differently. In that moment, I began to understand that this pain was not mine to carry. The recent interaction became an invitation, offering me a choice: to continue holding the emotional disconnect within my family as physical tension and quiet suffering, or to recognize the deeper grief I had been carrying for years, grief not for what our relationships were, but for what I had hoped they might become.

With that realization, something softened. I am different, yes, but not strange or flawed. I am authentic. I move through life with depth and heart, and that sensitivity has guided my purpose, my work, and the way I show up in the world. This way of being is welcomed in my adopted country, but it often disrupts the status quo of my culture of origin.

I also saw how often I had adjusted myself to fit what others could offer. I learned to dim my intuition, quiet my depth, and soften my knowing. When emotional clarity is mirrored back, it can stir discomfort in others. Without realizing it, I had learned to make myself smaller. I am no longer willing to do that.

As painful as the moment was, it reminded me of something essential:

I do not have to shrink to belong.
I do not have to silence myself to be accepted.
I do not have to carry the emotional limitations of others
as my own.

I can honor who others are while honoring who I am. I can love in the way I am built to love, even if only a few can meet me there. I have known deep connection, with Grace, who understood me without words, and with my mother, who saw me clearly in her later years. Those relationships remind me that I am not alone and never was.

This chapter of my life continues to call me back to myself. It asks me to honor my voice, my heart, and my way of moving through the world. It teaches me that not all paths are meant to merge, and that this does not diminish the value of each path.

What matters now is that I remain grounded in my authenticity, that I keep my heart open, even after hurt, and continue to understand, release, and grow. Each time I walk through moments like this, I step more fully into who I am. And that, in itself, is healing.

I am no longer hiding or reshaping myself to fit where I do not belong. I am growing into myself, embracing who I truly am, loving, intuitive, loyal, compassionate, humorous, and deeply connected to those who see my light. This is self-knowing. This is self-love. And perhaps, at last, this is self-acceptance.

Becoming Your Own Anchor

"The moment I realized I was my own anchor was the moment I stopped drifting and finally came home to myself."

For much of my life, I did not feel safe. This is something I have only recently been able to say out loud, not from a place of blame or resentment, but from clarity. On a quiet drive to work one morning, a powerful realization surfaced, I had been using other people as anchors to feel safe. Even more eye opening was the awareness that I no longer needed an anchor outside of myself. I recognized that I had become my own anchor.

For as long as I can remember, I looked to others to provide a sense of grounding and protection. I was naturally drawn to people who carried confidence, something I felt I lacked at the time. They were strong personalities, steady and assured, people I trusted would speak up when I could not. I leaned on them without fully realizing what I was doing. These "anchors" were never aware of the role I had assigned to them, yet energetically, I used them as my safe havens. I relied on their strength to steady me, their presence to make me feel protected, and their certainty to compensate for my own self-doubt. Looking back, I can see that what I was truly seeking was not their protection, but my own. I was borrowing confidence until I learned how to cultivate it within myself.

At the time, I did not recognize this pattern for what it truly was. I simply believed this was how life worked, that strength lived outside of me and safety came from attaching myself to others. It felt natural, even necessary.

Only now can I see that by anchoring myself to others, I was unknowingly placing myself in the background of my own life. By leaning on their confidence, their voices, and their strength, I kept myself beholden and quiet, not allowing my own power the space it needed to develop. What I experienced as protection was, in truth, a subtle form of self-abandonment.

I was not weak, I was learning. But until I stepped out from behind others, I could not fully discover my own voice, my own authority, or the strength that had always been waiting within me. My power was never absent, it was simply deferred, waiting for me to choose myself.

The need for safety did not come out of nowhere. It was shaped early on, rooted in experiences where I was not protected, not fully seen, and not truly heard. Growing up, I was surrounded by strong personalities, people who took up a lot of space. Maybe you have people in your life like that as well? Somewhere along the way, I learned to keep the peace. Whether that was a survival strategy or an act of self-preservation, I cannot say for certain, but I do know that in doing so, I slowly moved myself to the sidelines. To me, safety meant being able to let my guard down and be fully myself, without apology or fear of judgment. I believed this safety lived in others; in strong personalities I could lean on. Only later did I come to understand that true safety is not something another person can provide. It is something that must be cultivated within and needed to give myself.

That feeling stayed with me for decades. I adapted, adjusted, softened my edges, and learned how to read a room before speaking my truth. I changed myself in order to feel safe in any given situation. Safety of belonging became something I searched for externally instead of cultivating within. I did not realize that what I was truly longing for was not another person's strength, but my own. I was looking for places to belong in my life.

It took me more than fifty years to arrive at this understanding, and yet, the timing feels perfect. When the realization came, it did not arrive with anger or grief, but with relief. I no longer needed to attach myself to anyone to feel steady. I was no longer searching for something outside of me to make me feel whole. I had become my own anchor.

Being your own anchor does not mean you do not need others. It does not mean you close your heart or withdraw from connection. It means you stand firmly within yourself first. It means your sense of safety, worth, and direction comes from within, not from approval, protection, or validation outside of you. When you anchor into yourself, relationships change. You no longer cling, chase, or compromise your truth to belong. You choose connection from fullness rather than fear. You show up as you are, grounded, present, and whole.

Looking back now, I can see how long I lived without that inner safety. I can also see how much strength it took to survive without it. There is compassion in this awareness, not judgment. Every step I took led me here and it did not come without deep hurt and disconnection from people that I felt a safe connection with all my life, Today, I am no longer am willing to stand still on the sidelines but I am honoring the anchor in myself and pursuing activities that nourish my sense of wholeness.

If any of this feels familiar, know that there is nothing wrong with you. You are not behind, and you have not missed your moment. Understanding often comes slowly, unfolding only when we are ready to meet ourselves with honesty and compassion. Awakening often arrives quietly, in the middle of an ordinary moment, when we are finally ready to hear ourselves clearly.

Living Between Languages and Worlds

"You are allowed to belong to more than one place, more than one language, and more than one version of yourself."

Living between two cultures shapes you in ways that are often invisible to others. I often feel as though I stand with one foot in Holland and the other in the United States, yet I do not fully belong in either place. In Holland, I am often seen through an old lens, as the girl I once was, the one who spoke Dutch fluently and followed our cultural rules with ease. But I left decades ago, and for thirty-seven years the United States has shaped me into who I am today. My emotions, my thinking, and the way I express myself have expanded. And still, because I was not born here, there are moments when even my American family and colleagues misunderstand me.

I live between two countries, two languages, and two versions of myself. My roots are Dutch, but my branches grew in American soil. Because of that, several things have changed within me.

1. My language has shifted.
2. My sentence structure has changed.
3. My emotional communication has become more open.
4. My inner world has expanded far beyond the place
   I came from.

Each time I return to Holland, I try to reconnect with the version of myself my family remembers. I try to speak fluently, follow their rhythm, match their tone, and blend into the culture I once knew so well. But time changes you, and nearly four decades in another country make it impossible to fully step back into an old shape.

My effort often goes unnoticed and, at times, is even criticized. The Dutch tendency toward correctness and perfection means that my small mistakes in language or expression are often noticed more quickly than the intention behind my words, at times overshadowing what I am truly trying to communicate. And because my emotional openness does not align with a culture that values understatement, I once again feel out of place.

What touches me most is not the difference in language, but the space that sometimes exists emotionally. I find myself longing for small check-ins, casual conversations, and the simple moments that create a sense of closeness. Connection, when it flows naturally, feels nourishing to me. At times, that flow feels uneven. Contact often begins with me, and without that initiation, there is little exchange unless support or guidance is needed. I do not experience this as deliberate; it reflects a different way of relating rather than an absence of care. Still, the lack of those small gestures leaves a quiet loneliness within me, one that is not always easy to hold with compassion and often feels painful.

Because I connect through emotion, honesty, presence, and depth, the absence of those qualities affects me deeply. When these parts of me are not met, loneliness, and at times a quiet sense of betrayal, even in small doses, become part of my experience.

Yet there is strength in being shaped by two cultures. I carry two emotional languages, two ways of seeing the world, and a depth that was never meant to fit into a single box. That is the challenge, but it is also the gift. I can adapt, I can read different emotional climates, and I can draw wisdom from both sides of the world and offer it where it is needed.

What I have learned, slowly and with patience, is that I do not need to shrink my emotional strength because it makes others uncomfortable. My intuition is not an inconvenience. My softness is not a weakness. And although it may be frowned upon in Holland, my openness is not too much. It is simply who I am.

As I move forward, I honor that truth. I no longer need anyone to validate my existence. I am enough, exactly as I am. I have learned that I am worthy of being heard, and I honor my presence not only when I am alone, but also when I am surrounded by others.

On your own path, learn to honor your voice and live as your authentic self. Allow yourself the courage to speak from where you truly stand, even when your words feel different, even when they do not fit neatly into expectations. Discovering who you truly are is not only powerful, it is freeing. It releases the need to explain yourself, to shrink, or to translate your truth for the comfort of others. This is how change happens, not loudly or all at once, but steadily, one honest soul at a time.

When Others Misunderstand Your Light

"Your light is not meant to be understood by everyone. It is meant to guide those who are ready and release those who are not."

There came a moment in my journey when I began to recognize how my energy moved through the world. I noticed that people were drawn to me, that conversations softened and deepened in my presence, and that others often sought me out when they felt uncertain, overwhelmed, or in need of reassurance. This was never something I consciously tried to do, nor was it about fixing or saving anyone. It was simply a natural expression of who I am.

For those who feel called to be of service, the Lightworkers of the world, this awareness marks a quiet remembering, a recognition that your presence alone can offer steadiness, compassion, and hope in a world that deeply needs it. And yet, there are times when the very people who seek your guidance struggle to receive it. When insight touches places, they are not ready to explore, words can be misheard, intentions misunderstood, and care mistaken for judgment.

This chapter speaks to those moments. It is about recognizing what belongs to you and what does not. It is about honoring your gifts without taking responsibility for how others choose to receive them. It is also about releasing the guilt I carried surrounding my mother's final days and the family dynamics that unfolded around her passing.

For many years, I shared insights with an open heart. My guidance came from a place of care, honesty, and spiritual wisdom shared with me through universal sources. I never sought to be right, only to be helpful. Still, there were moments when my words were met not with understanding, but with rejection.

Within my family, this was especially painful. Advice offered with neutrality and respect was later described as unhelpful or hurtful, not because it lacked care, but because it asked for reflection. That realization touched something deep within me, especially given how much support I had offered over the years.

What I intended as empowerment was received differently. Encouragement was heard as judgment. Invitations toward self-trust and inner strength were perceived as distance rather than care. Watching the story shift as it was shared with others, particularly those I felt closest to, left me feeling unseen and deeply wounded.

This dynamic quietly carried into my final days with my mother. The sense of peace I had hoped for during that time was difficult to access. Our last in-person conversation was not centered on us, mother and daughter, but on unresolved emotions that did not belong to either of us. They stemmed from long-held trauma carried by a family member, a story that had resurfaced many times over the past twenty years. Once again, there was a strong need for that history to take center stage.

As differing perspectives emerged around how to address strained family relationships, the conversation became emotionally charged and difficult to settle that night. My mother did her best to be supportive, though she was already physically tired, and the emotional weight of it all made rest and sleep impossible for her.

When my mom and I said goodbye the next morning, she had not slept at all. I encouraged her to speak up, practice discernment, and clearly communicate that she would no longer engage in discussions about the matter moving forward. It was never my intention for this to be the focus of our final conversation, yet in that moment, my mother and I found ourselves shaped by the energy of another. As I kissed farewell on her cheeks, she held me close with her eyes, a quiet, deliberate presence, as if imprinting the moment into memory. I left shortly after for the airport, carrying her love with me, alongside the quiet weight of what had taken place. I had to release the guilt surrounding that moment. None of it was mine to carry, even though the sadness remains.

There were other moments when guidance offered in good faith was dismissed, minimized, or even turned into ridicule. These experiences were deeply painful, but they also revealed something essential, not everyone is ready to receive the light they ask for. Light cannot be forced, and insight cannot be received before the heart is ready.

Some people seek guidance because, on some level, they sense that you can see what they cannot. But when your truth touches places they avoid or have not yet healed, it becomes easier for them to project it back onto you. This may show up as anger, sarcasm, withdrawal, dismissal, or ridicule. Though it feels personal, their reactions are not about you. They are emotional defenses, attempts to protect themselves from what they are not ready to face.

The deeper lesson for me was learning when to give, when to step back, and when to protect my own heart. My light did not diminish. It simply required clearer boundaries. My intention remained pure, while their response reflected limitation.

There will always be people who misunderstand you. Their misunderstanding does not define your truth. Remember this:

- You are allowed to speak from your intuition.
- You are allowed to share your insight.
- You are allowed to protect your energy.
- You are allowed to walk away when your words are twisted.
- You are allowed to honor yourself.

Those who are truly ready will recognize your intention

immediately and receive your guidance for what it is, not control or judgment, but a quiet beacon of hope.

When people misunderstand you, it is not a punishment. It is an invitation to learn. These moments gently reveal where your energy no longer belongs, who is unable to meet you at the level you offer, and who may experience your light as a mirror they are not yet ready to face. They also show you where your boundaries are ready to strengthen and evolve. What may feel like rejection or confusion is often guidance, quietly redirecting you toward greater alignment, clarity, and self-respect.

With time, I came to see that none of these moments spoke to my worth or the truth of what I offered, though the feelings of hurt and betrayal needed space to heal. The deeper lesson in all of this is discernment, learning when to give, when to step back, and when to protect your own heart. Make sure your light remains steady and your intention pure, despite the limitations of others. Discernment is not about closing your heart, but about honoring it wisely so your energy is shared where it can truly be received.

Messages to the Universe

"The Universe listens to your energy, not your words.
Speak, think, and feel in harmony
with what you truly desire."

Recently, a client reminded me just how important it is to be conscious of the messages we send out to the Universe. If our thoughts and spoken words don't align with our true desires, the Universe has no choice but to respond to what we actually project outward and therefore ignore what we secretly wish for.

For example, if you want to build a relationship with someone romantic or otherwise, you must first open yourself up to receiving that connection. This means softening your defenses, releasing fear, and allowing yourself to be truly available to meet someone new.

How often do we hear someone say they want to find a partner, only to immediately list a set of requirements that this person must possess? The list might include ideal traits, but it often also contains dealbreakers. After meeting someone, they quickly decide that person falls short of their expectations and cut off any chance of connection. Without realizing it, they've already built walls around their heart.

When you speak those requirements aloud, you unintentionally limit the Universe's ability to surprise you. Your mental filter narrows your field of vision, and the Universe can only reflect your restrictions back to you. You may then feel frustrated, wondering why you keep attracting people who don't meet your standards, not realizing that you are the one shaping that pattern.

Instead, be aware of what you're projecting. Stay open, even if someone doesn't initially match your imagined ideal. You may be pleasantly surprised by what unfolds when you let go of rigid expectations and allow space for divine timing.

In my own life, I never expected that at twenty-one I would marry someone from another country and start a new life on a different continent, yet here I am. Because I didn't close myself off to the idea of being with someone from a different background, I said yes to love, got on a plane, and began a new chapter in California. That choice led to thirty-six years of marriage and two wonderful daughters. None of that would have happened if I'd stayed closed to new possibilities. I'm so grateful I was open to receiving those blessings. I believe the message I sent out to the Universe during that time was simple yet deeply rooted in trust. I believed that the world was far smaller than it appeared and that other cultures were not something to fear, but something to explore. To me, difference felt like adventure, not danger. I had an inner knowing that life expanded when you stepped beyond what was familiar, and that growth required movement, not comfort.

I also knew, without hesitation, that love was worth crossing oceans for. Leaving everything I knew behind and moving to the United States with my husband was not an act of recklessness, it was an act of faith. I trusted that love was not meant to confine me, but to guide me. Somewhere deep within, I sensed that this journey was part of my greater purpose, a necessary step toward discovering who I was meant to become.

Looking back now, I see that this decision was never just about geography. It was about alignment. I followed an inner pull that felt unmistakably right, even when logic could not fully explain it. By trusting that call, I stepped into my destiny. I did not lose myself by leaving my old life behind, I found myself by saying yes to what my soul already knew.

Be mindful of your words and your intentions. Words are powerful, they carry vibration and energy. The Universe is always listening and will respond accordingly. If you want a particular outcome, become conscious of your thoughts, your behavior, and your language. Everything is energy, and energy attracts its own kind. Choose your words intentionally, and you'll begin to attract people and experiences that align with your desires.

Once you become aware of this, you can attract anything you truly want into your life. In that way, you become more conscious of the messages you're sending out. The key is to match your energy to the energy of what you're seeking. It really is that simple. Everything is vibration, and everything is energy.

Matching your energy to what you desire isn't as difficult as it sounds. One of the most effective ways is through stillness, by sitting in silence and reflecting on your life. When anything feels tense or heavy, breathe and let it go. Allow yourself to settle into the frequency of peace, trust, and openness. This is how you create space for new things to enter your life. To receive, you must first release what no longer serves you, whether that's a physical object, a relationship, or a limiting belief. If it holds you back, bless it and let it go.

Letting go and manifesting are deeply connected. To bring something into your life, your energy must first meet it. In other words, your vibration has to align with what you wish to attract. This alignment doesn't come from forcing outcomes, but from doing the inner work, releasing what weighs you down, and creating space for something new to arrive.

Sometimes the Universe responds in small, almost playful ways, reminding us that we are being heard. I remember thinking about watching *Snow White*. The thought lingered for a while, even though I don't have a Disney subscription. Eventually, I let it go and moved on. A short time later, that exact version of *Snow White* appeared in my YouTube feed, available to watch for free. It may seem insignificant, but it was a clear reflection of how intention, when released without attachment, finds its way back to you.

Another experience showed up in a more meaningful way. I had been thinking about a coworker who might need support, but I hesitated. The situation felt delicate, and I didn't know how to approach her without causing discomfort. Rather than forcing the moment, I held the intention quietly and let it rest. A few days later, the perfect opening presented itself naturally, a conversation unfolded with ease, and the support I wanted to offer landed exactly as it was meant to.

These moments taught me something important. Manifestation begins with inner alignment. First, you must do the work of releasing fear, old trauma, and habitual responses that keep your vibration low. Then, you must be willing to let go and trust. Finally, you have to hold space, not gripping tightly, but remaining open enough for life to meet you halfway.

When you do the work, the Universe responds. Not always loudly or dramatically, but often in quiet, precise ways that remind you that you are supported, guided, and deeply connected. If you want happiness, change your thoughts and focus on what's already good in your life. If you want more abundance, make sure your thoughts reflect the abundance you currently have, even in the smallest of ways Begin by seeing yourself as abundant and open to possibility. Shift your energy toward inspired action, whether that means starting something new, taking small practical steps toward security, or cultivating gratitude for what already exists. These seemingly simple choices create meaningful shifts in your vibration and open the door for change.

Meditation is a wonderful tool to support this process. Set aside a few moments each day to sit quietly and listen within. Meditation is not about escaping the world but about returning to yourself. It's a sacred space to honor your journey, reflect on what serves you, and release what doesn't. Doing this can help you focus your thoughts on what you do want to create in your life. As you do, your vibration naturally rises, and life begins to flow more smoothly. The more you practice, the easier it becomes to shift your energy, and once you master that, you unlock the power to live the life you truly desire.

Wisdom and Tips from Beyond

*"The Universe always has perfect timing.
It reveals only what you're ready to receive,
never more, never less."*

Since my initial meditation almost twenty years ago, I have been fortunate to receive insights and guidance from multiple sources on the other side. I often refer to these beings as "Them" for lack of a better term. As I grew in my spirituality and expanded my awareness, these insights came more frequently and with greater depth, helping shape the person I am today.

During my thirties, I was struggling deeply in my relationship with my mother. I carried the belief that she did not love me or truly care for me. Almost immediately, the message I received was simple yet profound: she did love me, she just did not understand me. That insight shifted everything. From that moment on, I began to see our relationship through a different lens, one rooted in compassion rather than pain.

After my aunt passed away, I had an experience that stayed with me in a quiet but unmistakable way. My grandmother appeared to me gently, with her hands folded open as if offering something. Resting in her palms was a heart-shaped necklace. At the time, I didn't fully understand the meaning, only that it felt important and deeply intentional.

The next day, I shared this experience with my mother. She grew quiet and then told me she had bought that very heart necklace many years ago and had given it to my grandmother, who later passed it on to my aunt. When my mother shared this with my cousin, my aunt's daughter, she chose to wear the necklace to her mother's funeral after hearing what I had experienced. There was no way I could have known the history of that necklace. For me, this moment became a gentle but powerful reminder that our loved ones remain connected to us, finding ways to reach us through love, symbols, and meaning, even after we can no longer see them.

The most recent insight I received was a quiet but powerful reminder that everything comes back around. When you trust the process and have faith in the Universe, not every situation requires action. What I had initially perceived as rejection was shown to me from a different perspective, it was not rejection at all, but protection. The ego, when confronted with truth it is not ready to face, reacts defensively. It shields, deflects, and resists in order to maintain control. Understanding this brought a deep sense of peace. It allowed me to release the need to respond, justify, or explain. The ego is a strange yet powerful force, but once you recognize it for what it is, you no longer need to take its reactions personally. Everything unfolds in its own time, and clarity always finds its way back when you allow it to.

As you walk your own spiritual path, you will begin to recognize insights when they arrive. They may come as a sudden inner knowing, a line in a song that stops you in your tracks, an unexpected conversation, or even a scene in a movie that feels as though it was placed there just for you. When this happens, you don't question it, you feel it. Something resonates deeply, and you know the message is meant for you.

These insights do not arrive in the same way for everyone. Each of us receives guidance through the language we understand best. What matters is not how the message appears, but how it lands within you. My guidance is simple: do not rush these moments. Allow them to settle. Sit with them. Let their meaning unfold naturally over time.

These moments of clarity are not random. They come to guide you, to gently expand your awareness, soften your heart, and support the evolution of your soul. Each insight is an invitation to step more fully into who you already are and to trust the wisdom that is quietly revealing itself to you.

I believe that learning does not end with this physical life. Even after we transition from this world, there is still more to discover, more to explore, and more to understand. This belief was gently affirmed for me shortly after my father passed away. One day, I asked if he was all right on the other side. His response came immediately, not as a spoken voice, but as a clear feeling and an unmistakable sense of his presence. He conveyed that he was teaching there and that he loved it. What stood out most was his enthusiasm. He let me know, with warmth and certainty, that he had never been so busy.

Anyone who knew my father would recognize this instantly. Even while he was alive, especially after his retirement, he often joked that he had never been busier. Hearing that familiar expression again brought comfort, reassurance, and a quiet sense of continuity. It felt like him, fully himself, simply continuing his work in a different form. That moment reminded me to always stay open to growth, new perspectives, and the ever-expanding wisdom that surrounds us.

Trust that the Universe has extraordinary things in store for you. All you have to do is stay present, stay curious, and stay open. The Universe always has perfect timing. It reveals only what you are ready to receive, never more, never less. If too much information arrived at once, it would overwhelm you, and you would most likely shut down. Trust that the right information will reach you at exactly the right time. That is where expansion takes place, and that is where you find happiness.

A Touch of Divine Grace

"When grace touches you, it doesn't ask for explanation,
it simply awakens something deep within your soul."

On January 28th, 2021, I had the profound experience of being visited by Jesus. Just before going to sleep, He appeared to me in a vision. While He stood in front of me, he gently touched my forehead with His finger. Although I still don't know why He appeared to me, I do believe that it was for a divine purpose. He was dressed all in white, His aura radiating with a brilliant, cloaked light. The entire encounter lasted only a couple of minutes, but I can recall every detail with clarity. All I can say is that I felt invited, accepted, and deeply loved, and I am eternally grateful for the visit.

Two months later, I was diagnosed with Stage 3 colon cancer. Some might think that His appearance was somehow connected, but I believe that His touch gave me the strength to endure and overcome what was to come. I felt like his visit was him telling me that I would be okay and survive, which I did. I underwent surgery and chemotherapy, and although difficult, I never gave up hope. Four years later, I remain in remission and am so grateful to be alive.

Seeing Jesus was not new to me. Over the years, during many meditations, I had felt the presence of both Jesus and God. This encounter, however, was different. He appeared suddenly and without any prompting, as if to reassure me in that exact moment that I would be okay. There was no message delivered in words, only a deep, quiet knowing. I believe this was an act of grace, arriving precisely when I needed strength the most. It awakened something within me, a remembrance of faith, trust, and divine support that carried me forward when my own strength felt limited.

You might wonder, why I've had so many encounters with the beyond, "Why me?" I can't give you a definitive answer. What I can say is that I've released enormous amounts of negativity, self-doubt, and self-sabotage over the years. I've forgiven those who trespassed on my boundaries. I've come to know myself and have cultivated a deep sense of self-respect. I've become a stronger version of myself, one who walks into the world with an open heart and mind.

These encounters gently affirmed the decisions I made to no longer carry old trauma and anger with me. They helped me build trust in myself and in the quiet strength that comes from living authentically. Each experience felt like a subtle sign along the way, encouraging me to let go of people, dynamics, and situations that no longer resonated with my energy. The message was always the same, steady and reassuring, keep shining, stay true to who you are, and don't make yourself smaller to be accepted. By listening to that guidance, I stepped more fully into myself, and in doing so, I discovered a deeper sense of freedom.

These moments are not reserved for a chosen few. They are available to anyone willing to live with awareness, integrity, and courage. When you learn to listen, release what no longer serves you, and trust your inner guidance, you step into alignment with who you truly are. From that alignment, clarity unfolds, your path becomes visible, and the next chapter of your journey begins to reveal itself.

Honoring Love Through Loss

*"Love never dies. It transforms, it expands,
and it continues to guide us in ways
that words can't describe."*

Some people shape your life so profoundly that even after they're gone, their presence lingers softly but unmistakably in the background. My mother and my dear friend Grace are two of those people. Like an invisible thread running through my days, their love continues to guide me.

My bond with my mother was one of the most cherished connections in my life. Especially in her later years, as we grew closer than ever. I would travel every six months from the U.S. to the Netherlands to spend time in my ancestral home. During the day, we each followed our own rhythm, but in the evenings, we slipped into a beautiful ritual. I would cook dinner, we'd eat side by side with our plates on little trays in front of the TV watching the news, and after my evening walk, we'd share tea and chocolates from the shop down in the village while diving into long, meaningful conversations. We discussed everything. Nothing was off topic. That in itself is rare and is witness to our closeness. The last time I saw and spoke with her in person, she thanked me profusely for all the meaningful conversations we shared.

I treasure those quiet hours together. My mother was wise, strong, and resilient. She had survived a Japanese prison camp during World War II and lived with the quiet challenge of dyslexia, which made her self-conscious, yet it never diminished her ability to lead with love and insight. She remained the matriarch of our family until her very last breath, always listening, always holding space.

Some of her wise words still reside within me:

"Child, everyone is different, and the strength lies in how to get along with everyone "and
"Things will always work out differently than you imagine."

These messages were her legacy, truths she lived and passed on without needing to preach. In her presence, I felt seen and at home. I felt at peace within our relationship and am thankful for the beautiful memories I have, I cherish them. I honor her love by allowing it to continue shaping how I live, how I listen, and how I move through the world. Even in her absence, her wisdom remains present, guiding me with quiet strength and reminding me that love does not end, it transforms.

Then there was Grace.

Our friendship spanned over thirty years. Grace was unlike anyone else, quirky, expressive, and warm. She could make me laugh like no other, but we also sat together in our tears. Over the decades, we weathered many storms side by side, holding each other through life's heartbreaks. Around Grace, I never had to perform or pretend. I could simply be.

Our conversations began the moment I picked her up from her house, so rich and immediate that I sometimes needed to stop the car just to decide where we were going for lunch. It didn't matter how long we'd gone without speaking. When we came back together, it was as if no time had passed.

Grace had an immense capacity to love, even though that love wasn't always returned in the way she deserved. Still, she gave generously, from her heart, from her time, even financially, despite not having much herself. She had a unique way of telling stories, full of drama, animated and delightful. She had a love and sweetness that always wrapped me in care. She knew I loved hummingbirds and, over the years, gifted me a mug, earrings, and a bracelet, all small treasures that now carry her energy. More importantly, she sent me a sign shortly after she passed. While working in my backyard, I turned toward the fountain and noticed a hummingbird appear seemingly out of nowhere. Its coloring was a striking blue; deeper and more vivid than the hummingbirds I usually see in my garden. It was also larger, and instead of darting away as they typically do, it hovered quietly about a foot in front of me, remaining there for several minutes. I stood completely still, aware that this was not an ordinary moment. In all my years of watching hummingbirds, I had never experienced anything like it. In that stillness, I felt her presence clearly, gentle, reassuring, and unmistakably close.

Every time we parted ways, she would say, "I love you, be safe and I will pray for you," and she always meant it. Her love was a prayer in motion, one that to this day, continues to bless me. I honor Grace by living fully, by honoring my own voice, and by choosing kindness and openness, the way she always did. She was generous with her time, her presence, and her heart, always willing to listen, always ready to help, giving freely without expectation or condition. That was simply who she was.

She carried an angelic quality in the way she moved through the world, offering love even when it was not returned in kind. In honoring her, I also choose to honor myself, in the ways she was not always able to. I live more consciously, more truthfully, and more gently, carrying forward the love she embodied and allowing it to continue through me.

These two women, my mother and my friend, held different spaces in my life and unfortunately, I lost both of them within the same year. These women taught me about the depth and endurance of unconditional love. They are part of the spiritual team that surrounds me now. When I light a candle, when I sit quietly, when I reach into my heart and listen, I can still feel them there. Their love didn't end, it simply changed form and it stays with me, always. Although I lost their physical presence, I never lost their love. I honor that love by carrying their memories within me, always present, always guiding me.

Becoming Me Through It All

*"I didn't become myself in spite of my struggles;
I became myself because of them."*

The events that have shaped me into the person I am today are many, some beautiful and others difficult and hard to overcome. But I carry them all with me. Without those experiences, I don't believe I would be the strong, loyal, spiritual, stubborn, and yes, still fiercely independent person I am now.

These days, I balance the many roles that are part of me. I care for my family and pets, work my regular job, make time for friends, and run a monthly Reiki circle. I also offer private Reiki healing sessions and mediumship readings. I continue to explore, learn, and grow, because I believe personal growth never stops. I find myself more and more in tune with the messages I receive from spiritual sources and loved ones who have crossed over, and I no longer hide from their messages. Their guidance helps me navigate the present and allows me to help others when they find themselves stuck. I hold firmly the belief that learning never ends, and that we should always remain open to new possibilities. Some of the lessons I've learned, however, have been far from easy. I've had times when I doubted everything, the people around me, the Universe, even myself. Anger, betrayal, loss and sorrow have all been part of the process. I've questioned why certain things had to happen, or what I might have done differently. Still, in the long run, I never stray too far from my belief in Source. That connection runs deep, and even in my most uncertain moments, it quietly remains and has been instrumental in becoming who I am today.

I've come to understand that in order to support and guide others, I must first live through my own struggles. I need to feel the weight of loss, confusion, or disappointment before I can speak honestly about how to move through them. The more I've walked though, the more I can offer. In this way, life becomes both a teacher and a gift. Authenticity doesn't come from theory; it comes from firsthand experience. People feel it in your voice, your energy, and your words, and that validates your message of hope.

At 58, I'm still becoming who I'm meant to be. As my husband and I continue to grow in our relationship, we become closer not only as a couple, but also as individuals. I grow into my role within the family, not just as a mother or partner, but as myself. For a long time, I put everyone else's well-being before my own. I know many women will recognize themselves in that. Today, I am finally giving myself the time and attention I once chose to forgo. That doesn't mean I ignore the needs of those I love. It simply means I honor my own needs too. I make decisions more mindfully and choose how to spend my energy more wisely and with greater care.

Although both of my daughters have moved out, they continue to come home regularly. Each visit brings its own quiet lesson, often unexpected, yet always meaningful. One of the hardest lessons I've learned as a mother is knowing when to step back and trust that they will find their own way. Over time, I've come to understand that love does not mean holding on, it means allowing. I remind myself that they need to live their own lives, face their own challenges, and make their own choices in order to grow into who they are meant to be. It isn't easy. Every part of me wants to help, to fix, to guide. Yet I've learned that releasing control is an act of trust, and that trusting them is also trusting life itself. Holding on too tightly would only keep them from discovering their own strength.

I have a beautiful life filled with love, family, and friendship. But that life has not come without trials and tribulations. Like many, I've faced loss, illness, betrayal, heartache, and moments of depression. In order to find my voice and sense of self, I've had to go deep within, facing parts of my past I once wanted to avoid. Some wounds go back to early childhood. My trust was broken by people who should have protected me, and it took me many years to heal. But with the support of therapy, Reiki, family, and friends, I've made tremendous progress and can now enjoy the fruits of my labor, letting go of what no longer serves me.

Although there were moments when I wanted to give up, I didn't. I found an inner strength I didn't know I had. And that's something I want to remind you of you are much stronger than you think. Our minds have a life of their own and can become our greatest enemy when we allow fear or hopelessness to settle in. That energy is heavy and difficult to overcome. But when we shift our thoughts, even slightly, we change the direction of our lives. That shift matters. It's a life changer, the beginning of something new that opens the door to fresh possibilities.

These days, I focus more on being in the moment. I find comfort in the present, not because everything is perfect, but because I've stopped trying to control what I can't. I allow things to unfold in their own time. I recently heard someone say that nature has its own rhythm, and I believe we've forgotten how to live by it. In the natural world, letting go is not a loss but a quiet act of trust. Trees release their leaves each fall, knowing spring will return. Rivers shift and reshape their path, allowing the water to find its way. Nature doesn't cling; it listens and adjusts. There is a wisdom in that, a reminder that we, too, are meant to evolve, soften, and let life carry us where we are meant to go. Nothing stays the same, and neither do we. Nor should we. It is important to allow change to shape the direction of our life. Without it, we become complacent and unwilling to move forward.

Letting go of the old hasn't always been easy for me. My ego likes to cling to what's familiar. But I'm learning. I don't know what the future holds, and surprisingly, I'm okay with that. Just like a tree stands bare in winter, waiting for spring to arrive, I too am learning to trust the cycle. We are always in the process of growing, releasing, and renewing. Life moves in seasons, and so do we. I believe I will continue to evolve as a person. The choices I make each day will shape what comes next. Small or large, those choices matter. I trust that the lessons, reflections, and wisdom I've shared bring you comfort, and that they offer your insight and guidance as you walk your own path. My wish is that they help you trust yourself more deeply and guide you to make choices that support the life you truly want to live.

What is Next

*"It is now or never; you either accept that you have to change
or decide to remain the same.
The choice is yours!"*

Each of us walks a unique path. How you move forward and what your next step looks like is a choice only you can make. The guidance that leads you there may arrive gently, quietly, or at times with greater urgency, because the Universe meets each of us where we are. No two journeys are the same. Our interests, values, goals, and life circumstances shape who we become, moment by moment. In that way, we are formed by the sum of our experiences, our thoughts, our emotions, and the choices we make along the way.

Although it's impossible to know exactly what lies ahead, it is only natural to pause and wonder what comes next. The following guidelines are suggestions to help you discover what might work for you. Take time to reflect and trust your inner voice. If something doesn't resonate or feel right, let it go. If something speaks to you, embrace it, explore it to truly understand the concept, work with it, and watch the change unfold before you.

It is now or never. You either accept that you have to change, or you decide to remain the same. The choice is yours. But to become the best version of yourself, you must let go of the old and welcome the new. This begins with you.

For me, this turning point unfolded over many years through a series of defining moments. Moment 1: not feeling seen or truly heard within my family. Moment 2: feeling and sensing the world more intensely than others and learning to accept it instead of letting it diminish me. Moment 3: receiving insights and visits from light beings and spiritual figures that affirmed a deeper truth. Moment 4: finding a career that allowed me to use my sensitivity in service of healing others. Moment 5: leaving my home country to begin a new life with my husband, trusting love and purpose enough to leap. And finally, receiving a cancer diagnosis that asked everything of me and changed me forever.

Each moment invited me to choose growth over fear and truth over comfort. Together, they led me back to myself, and they taught me that returning to who you are is not passive, it asks for your participation. Not through force or urgency, but through honest reflection and a willingness to grow.

There comes a point when the path forward asks for your participation. Not through force or urgency, but through honest reflection and willingness to grow. This begins by turning inward and taking stock of who you are becoming. Notice your strengths, acknowledge where resistance still lives, and listen for what brings you a genuine sense of meaning and aliveness. These are the places where your energy naturally wants to move, quietly guiding you forward.

From that awareness, intentions begin to form. They don't have to be grand or perfectly defined. What matters is that they feel true to you. Some steps will be small, others more daring, but each one carries value. There is no perfect timing, only the moment you decide to begin.

Along the way, support will appear, sometimes through people who offer insight, encouragement, or a perspective you hadn't considered. Growth does not happen in isolation, and allowing yourself to learn from others does not diminish your strength, it deepens it.

When clarity arrives, even quietly, action follows. Not rushed or forced, but steady. Progress unfolds one step at a time. You may not always see where it leads, but trust builds through movement, not waiting. As you go, remain open. Life often responds in ways you couldn't have planned.

Change is part of this unfolding. Expansion asks you to step beyond what feels familiar and to loosen your attachment to old ways of being. This is where growth lives, at the edge of comfort, where your light stretches and finds new expression.

And as life continues to shift, so will you. Pause often. Reflect. Adjust when needed. The path is not linear, and it was never meant to be. With time, perspective widens, and you begin to see how each choice, each moment of courage, carried you forward.

This is not about becoming someone else. It is about remembering who you are, and allowing that truth to guide you, gently and consistently, from within.

You are a unique individual, and only you know what is best for you. It is essential that you listen to your intuition, follow your heart, and make choices you can live with. Trust yourself, both in what you face and, in your ability, to create a meaningful, fulfilling life.

In Part 2, I'll share some tangible ways you can begin to live this more fully. You don't need to have everything figured out. Start with one small step, make one conscious change, and stay consistent. Remain open, and trust that your life can grow into something beautiful, starting right where you are.

As I close this part of my journey, I feel deep gratitude for how far I've come and for everything I've learned along the way. Each experience, joyful or painful, has shaped me into who I am today. Growth does not end; it simply evolves as we do.

The next part of this book invites you to journey inward and upward, to connect more deeply with the guidance that has always surrounded you. It is a space where the spiritual and the everyday meet, where messages from higher realms offer clarity, comfort, and truth.

If you soften your mind and open your heart, you may begin to sense the love and wisdom that are always available to you. Together, we'll explore what it means to trust that guidance, to listen more deeply, and to remember that you are never alone on this path. Take a breath, open your heart, and step with me into Part 2.

Part 2

MESSAGES FROM BEYOND:
AUTHOR'S NOTE ON PART 2

Before moving into the second part of this book, I want to pause and acknowledge the path that has brought you here. Everything you've read so far has asked you to look at yourself and your life and be open to new awareness and opportunities to connect with yourself. honestly, gently, and without judgment. It has invited you to understand the patterns that formed you, the emotions that shaped you, and the ways you learned to protect yourself long before you even knew you were doing it.

The chapters in the first section were written to help you recognize yourself, meaning the version of you that has been shaped by years of experiences, beliefs, expectations, and survival strategies. They were meant to help you see how much of your inner world was formed long before you were old enough to make sense of it.

As you move into the next part of this book, you enter a different kind of space. The teachings ahead do not ask you to accept a single truth, nor do they claim to hold the ultimate answers. Instead, they serve as gentle reminders; see them as invitations rather than instructions. They are here to help you reconnect with the part of yourself that already knows, the part of you that remembers what your mind may have forgotten.

What you will read next comes from a quieter place, a deeper knowing, one that speaks softly yet powerfully when we allow ourselves to listen. It is a space where life is not something to analyze, but something to feel. A space where wisdom doesn't come from effort, but from allowing.

This section of the book is meant to support you as you shift from understanding yourself to meeting yourself, the truest, clearest version of who you are beneath all the layers. Part 2 is meant to bridge human experience with the spiritual one, reminding you that healing doesn't only happen by looking back, but also by opening up to what flows through you now. If the first part of this book helped you see how your old wounds were formed, this second part helps you remember who you are beyond them. It offers guidance from a higher perspective, yet remains grounded in real life, honesty, and the everyday moments where transformation truly happens.

As my own journey continues, I am discovering that healing does not end with understanding the past. Once we make peace with the past, we are no longer bound by it, and new layers of understanding begin to reveal themselves. For me, this unfolded in the form of being called to look beyond the physical world, to listen to the subtle guidance that had always been around me. In quiet moments, in stillness, in meditation, I began receiving messages from a deeper source, from energies that speak to the part of us that has always known more than the mind can explain. These teachings are not bound by time or place, and they are not here to impose a truth. They are here to spark remembrance, to encourage reflection, and to offer support to anyone who feels ready to explore what lies beneath the surface of everyday life.

The chapters ahead gather the wisdom that arrived in quiet moments when I was open and listening. They are shared with love, offered by the spiritual sources, guides, and loved ones who continue to walk beside me, and shaped by my own experiences as I learn and grow. Some of their words may feel familiar, as if they echo thoughts, you've held quietly within yourself. Others may nudge you to see things from a different angle or invite you to look at your life, your choices, or even your own heart with new understanding.

Use what supports you and feels right where you are in your life and let go of anything that doesn't fit your journey right now. Each of us is different and unique, and, what works for one will not necessarily work for another. Let these teachings meet you exactly where you are and most of all, trust yourself as you move forward.

Part 2 is meant to be a companion you can return to again and again. It is not designed to be read from beginning to end, but to be opened when you feel called. Think of it as daily guidance, something you can turn to in the morning before the world begins pulling at your attention.

You may open to any page and trust that what you land on holds something for you in that moment. There is no right order, no sequence to follow. Simply allow the message to meet you where you are and let it gently guide your day. Trust that whatever you read is what you are meant to receive in that moment.

These teachings are not here to tell you what to believe. They are here to help you remember what your soul already knows. Take what resonates, leave what does not, and return whenever your heart calls you back.

Let us begin.

Getting to Know Your Ego

The ego is part of your identity. It lives in your thoughts and plays a key role in how you interact with the world. Its primary function is survival. In situations of danger, it activates your fight-or-flight response and works to keep you safe. In that sense, the ego can serve a vital purpose. But when you're not in actual danger, when you're trying something new, changing a habit, or stepping outside your comfort zone, the ego often becomes an obstacle rather than a defender.

Once you become aware of your ego, you begin to realize that it has a mind of its own. I sometimes refer to it as the "Chihuahua voice", meaning the one that never stops yapping. It jumps from thought to thought without warning, feeds on drama, insecurity, and control. Have you ever had a negative encounter that lingers in your mind far longer than it should? That's your ego at work. Once it latches onto something, it runs wild, and it can take real effort to override it.

When your ego becomes dominant, it drowns out everything else. It's hard for messages from your higher self to break through. To make things worse, thoughts filtered through the ego are often laced with fear, anger, or doubt. In contrast, your higher self speaks from a place of calm clarity, love, and deep inner knowing. But to access it, you need intention, awareness, and practice.

This process is not always easy, and there is no one-size-fits-all approach. For some, especially those shaped by trauma or deeply ingrained patterns, retraining the mind can take time. The most important step is simply this, do not remain stuck in the energy of drama. Drama feeds the ego, and when you stay there, forward movement becomes difficult.

Forgiveness is essential on this path, not for the person who hurt you, but for your own freedom. Forgiveness releases the heaviness that keeps you tethered to the past. Without it, progress often stalls. When the moment to forgive arrives, you will feel it in your body and your spirit. Trust that inner knowing. You will recognize when the time is right.

One way to begin quieting the ego is by slowing your breath and becoming aware of where in your brain your thoughts are most active. Notice when the "Chihuahua voice" is speaking. See if you can gently move those thoughts to the background and make space for something deeper to emerge.

You may notice that the ego voice feels fast, analytical, and restless, often located toward the front of the mind. Messages from the higher self, on the other hand, may feel as though they arise from the center or back of the mind, or even from the heart space. Pay attention during meditation, stillness, or quiet reflection. For me, higher messages often come when I am fully present and still, and I feel the area behind my right ear subtly activated. Over time, you too can learn to consciously shift your awareness from one voice to the other.

The more often you choose to listen to your higher self, the easier it becomes. As this connection strengthens, your actions begin to change, not only toward yourself, but also in how you relate to others. Compassion grows more naturally. Judgment softens. You begin to live with greater intention and gentleness.

Once you learn the difference, the contrast between the ego and the higher self becomes clearer. Ego-based thoughts tend to be reactive and judgmental, especially toward yourself. The higher self speaks with understanding and love. It sees beyond appearances and recognizes energy and essence. When the ego says, "I don't like that person," the higher self gently asks, "What might they be carrying that I don't see?" or simply reminds you that everyone is on their own journey.

With awareness and practice, you can begin to change your thoughts midstream. That's where real power lies, in your ability to interrupt destructive patterns so you can choose differently. It takes effort at first to interrupt your familiar reactive thought patterns. However, the more you do it, the more natural it becomes.

You might wonder why we even need the ego, especially if it seems to bring so much negativity. The ego does have a role. It helps you function in our physical world. It provides structure and identity. The goal is not to eliminate the ego, but to keep it in balance. When left unchecked, the ego tends to spiral into overdrive. It thrives on drama, rehearses old stories, reinforces negative thought patterns, and replays difficult situations endlessly. These mental loops can affect your health by causing stress, sleeplessness, anxiety, and even illness.

That is why paying attention to your thoughts each day is so important. Notice their tone. Ego chatter is often critical, fearful, or doubtful. The voice of the higher self, by contrast, carries reassurance, acceptance, and love. Begin to lean toward that gentler voice. With time, you will feel the difference, not only in your thoughts, but in how you live.

Train your mind to identify when the ego is talking and then gently guide your thoughts. To begin recognizing when the ego is speaking, try this:

- When a thought feels urgent, fearful, or judgmental, pause and take a slow breath. Ask yourself, *"Is this fear, or is this truth?"* Awareness alone begins the shift.
- When the inner voice becomes critical or loud, respond with kindness. Silently say, *"I see you, but I choose differently,"* and redirect your attention to your breath, your body, or something grounding.

As you practice this, alignment with your higher self becomes more natural. You'll notice how life begins to respond in subtle, unexpected ways. Align with your higher self and see what unfolds. Life is an adventure, and the Universe often surprises us when we least expect it. Let's go and live your life fully. The choice is yours, and you are capable. I believe in you.

You'll know when the ego no longer runs the show, life begins to open. You experience greater peace, clarity, and possibility. Doubt and self-judgment loosen their grip. You feel stronger and more connected to your inner guidance and better equipped to navigate whatever comes your way.

Let go of the ego and live your life fully. The choice is yours, and you are capable.

Reflection

- Where do you notice your "Chihuahua voice" showing up most often in your day?
- How does your body feel when your ego is in control versus when your higher self is guiding you?
- What practices help you reconnect to your higher self-most easily, stillness, breath, nature, or something else?

Affirmation

"I recognize my ego, but I am guided by my higher self. I release drama, embrace peace, and walk in love and awareness."

Clearing Your Mind

The ego mindset is one of the most persistent forces in our lives, often keeping us in a state of inner conflict and imbalance. Its primary mission is survival. To fulfill that mission, the ego attaches itself to whatever it can energetically feed on, a person, an event, or a belief. Much like a parasite, it continues to draw energy until it is satisfied or finds something new to cling to. The ego thrives on drama, and the more attention and emotion we give it, the stronger it becomes.

When we begin to release our attachment to the ego, our minds naturally become clearer. A clear mind allows for conscious, grounded decision-making. Until that clarity is established, it is important to stay alert and to question our thoughts, decisions, and actions. Many people act on their thoughts automatically, without ever pausing to ask where those thoughts originate. This inner investigation is essential if you wish to free yourself. Ask yourself, where do your thoughts come from? Are they shaped by your parents, your culture, your community, or past trauma? Are you repeating patterns that no longer serve you simply because they are familiar? All these influences can linger beneath the surface and quietly guide your behavior.

Change begins by examining and clearing your thoughts. Since all action begins with thought, it is the mind that must be addressed first. This work is not easy, and it cannot be done for you. Only you have access to your inner landscape. Only you know what feels true and what no longer fits. Consider this when making decisions, are my decisions driven by fear, love, or conditioned thinking? While outside resources such as books, workshops, or teachers can be helpful, they are only tools. Ultimately, you are the one who must apply the tools and do the work of reshaping your inner mind. what resonates. The answers you are seeking already live within you, waiting to be seen and acknowledged.

To free the mind from ego-driven patterns and reach deeper awareness, inner work is required. This process is often referred to as shadow work. It does not mean confronting everything at once. It means beginning honestly and gently, one step at a time. Patience, self-honesty, and discernment are essential here. When the process is rushed, the mind can become overwhelmed and shut down, making it harder to move forward. With steady observation and conscious choice, the ego mindset can be transformed, and life begins to be seen through a clearer, more empowered lens.

As this process unfolds, your authentic self naturally comes forward. You may feel more grounded, more confident, and more capable of responding rather than reacting. With clarity, your choices begin to reflect not only your own highest good, but the well-being of others as well. The ego is always self-serving, whereas the higher self is inclusive, aiming to help others. This is where transformation begins, both individually and collectively.

Before moving on, take time to reflect on the questions below. Take some time with these questions. See which one seems to speak to you right now. Answering too many at once can activate the ego's defenses and lead to overwhelm. Move slowly and integrate one question at a time into your daily life. Progress is not linear. If you fall back, begin again. This journey is not about reaching a destination, but about honoring the process and trusting yourself along the way.

I often compare this process to staring college. If you were handed four years' worth of material on the first day, you would likely feel defeated before you even began. Yet when you approach it one class and one semester at a time, it becomes manageable. The same applies here. Small, steady steps allow the mind to clear and make space for higher wisdom to enter.

Reflection Questions
1. What thoughts occupy my mind most often?
2. Where does this thought originate?
3. Is this thought true? Does it still hold value for me?
4. Is this conditioned thinking influenced by others, such as my parents, culture, or community?
5. What feels true to me at this moment?
6. Does my ego voice always tell me the truth?
7. Do I act primarily from fear or from love?
8. What are my weak points, and am I willing to improve or release them?
9. What is holding me back?
10. How do I envision a new and more aligned version of myself?
11. What actions can I take today to create different results?
12. What keeps me from taking those actions? Why do I sabotage myself?
13. After making changes, what results do I notice?
14. How do I maintain this new energy?
15. Can I let go of what no longer serves me? If not, what holds me there?

The Universe is always offering guidance and support, but the ego can interfere. It may whisper, "This isn't real," or "You're imagining things." This is where discernment becomes essential. You get to choose which voice you listen to.

You may be familiar with the Native American story of the two wolves, one representing light and the other darkness. When asked which wolf wins, the answer is simple, the one you feed. Feed your higher self. Create space for silence, insight, and divine guidance. Allow your thoughts to evolve and let your life reflect the transformation that follows.

Reflection Practice

- Choose one of the fifteen questions above. Spend three mornings journaling for five to ten minutes on that single question. When your mind wants to rush the answer, pause and ask, is this my truth, or someone else's?
- Practice a gentle breath check. When the "Chihuahua voice" appears, inhale for four counts, hold for two, exhale for six. Repeat three times and notice what softens.

Affirmation

"I notice my thoughts without judgment. I choose the voice of my higher self and act from love, clarity, and balance."

The Dark Side of Humanity

We each process two sides within us, our shadow self and what we might call our angelic self. This duality mirrors the duality of the world we live in. Modern life bombards us with negativity and often leaves us wondering why we suffer, why wars persist, and why injustice prevails. Turn on the news or scroll through social media and it becomes clear how much division exists. These experiences are not random. They are expressions of human consciousness, though not always its highest expression.

Beyond our earthly experience, beyond the veil, there is only love. I know this, because I have felt it firsthand. We come into this life with a soul blueprint: an intention for what we want to learn and experience. Free will allows us to choose how those lessons unfold. We can meet them with awareness and grace, or we can resist them and learn through pain. When guidance is ignored, the lessons often repeat, not as punishment, but as an invitation to awaken and grow. Personal growth rarely happens without challenge, because comfort can easily lead to stagnation.

Each of us carries a dark side within. It may lie dormant for years, but eventually it surfaces, often triggered by deeply buried emotions or unresolved experiences. When this happens, it can feel unsettling, even overwhelming. You may experience a sudden shift and feel as though you no longer recognize yourself. This is not something to fear.

No one is exempt from having a shadow. What matters is not its presence, but how we relate to it. Healing does not come from fighting ourselves, but from working with what arises. Do not run from it or suppress it. Instead, acknowledge these emotions as part of your human experience. The shadow loses its power when it is seen and accepted. Letting go is a gradual process that requires patience and self-compassion. The ego often resists this work, clinging to what is familiar, even when that familiarity is painful. Yet change is possible.

As long as we remain trapped in ego-driven beliefs such as "I am right," "I am better," or "you are wrong," division continues. Breaking this cycle begins with reflection and conscious choice. When we learn to master our emotions rather than be ruled by them, we create space to act from our higher self instead of reacting from ego. This is where meaningful change begins.

When we change our thoughts, our behavior follows. When our behavior changes, our lives begin to transform. Many people are already awakening to this truth. Evolution is rarely fast, but over time, sustained inner work leads to lasting change. With enough awareness and intention, future generations can inherit a more conscious and compassionate world.

So, what are some ways to address our shadow selves? In moments of anger or despair, pause before reacting. Breathe. Observe what is happening within you. The ego may push for immediate reaction, but your breath can anchor you. Take 3-5 breaths. From that place of presence, you can respond not from fear, but from wisdom. A single conscious response has a ripple effect, touching those around you and inviting them to choose differently as well.

. When you change, others feel it. We are all energetically connected When you act in alignment, it uplifts not only you, but the collective as a whole. You are capable and powerful, continually evolving as you move forward. So, breathe deeply and observe your thoughts. Master your emotions and you become part of the positive change. and choose to be the change forward.

Reflection

- What emotions or traits do I find hardest to accept in myself?
- When do I notice my shadow appearing — and how do I usually respond?
- How can I bring compassion instead of judgment to the darker parts of myself?
- This week, try pausing before reacting in one difficult moment. Notice the difference between ego's impulse and your higher self's guidance.

Affirmation

"I face my shadow with courage and compassion."
"I am whole, balanced, and guided by love."

Responding to Hurt

Throughout life, we will face moments where your feelings are hurt. We all encounter, at times, negative situations, difficult people, or unsettling news. What defines the depth of your hurt is not the event itself, but how we respond to it.

The intensity of that hurt depends on the emotions we attach to the situation. Some experiences cut deep, while others barely leave a mark. What makes the difference?

It is our level of attachment to the situation. Too often, we add to our own suffering by assigning harsh meaning to someone's words or actions, reacting immediately, and therefore amplifying our stress. The problem lies in that we see everything through our own filter, which means we assign the meaning, not the person who confronted us.

You hold the power to decide how much pain you experience. Rather than reacting blindly to each situation, you can choose to pause, step back from the surge of emotions, and approach the moment with clarity. When you allow yourself to reflect before reacting, you regain your power. From a broader perspective, a bird's-eye view, you can respond with wisdom rather than impulse. In doing so, you lessen the sting of the moment and reclaim control over your emotions.

This does not mean you will never feel hurt again. Loss, grief, insults or the passing of a beloved pet will still affect you deeply. Sometimes, it only takes an unkind remark or a disregard for our boundaries to awaken pain we thought we had moved beyond. Yet even in these moments, reflection and acceptance allow healing to come more gently. Before you can release hurt, begin with two simple steps. First, pause and honestly name what you are feeling, whether it is anger, disappointment, sadness, or grief. Naming the emotion brings it into awareness and prevents it from quietly controlling your reactions.

Second, allow yourself to feel the emotion in your body without rushing to fix, explain, or suppress it. Sit with it briefly. Notice where it lives within you. Give it space to be acknowledged. When you approach your pain in this way, it begins to soften. By recognizing the experience for what it is, rather than resisting it, you move through it with greater ease and gradually find your way forward.

Hurt is part of life, but you are not powerless against it. The choice lies in how you respond, how you allow it to shape you, and how quickly you release it. Choose wisely. Take charge of your emotions, and you will discover that even hurt doesn't have to live with you for your whole life. Instead, these experiences can offer the opportunity to process and make choices over what you let control you. In this way, hurt can transform into growth, strength, and wisdom. The wisdom we gain from reflecting on our hurtful experiences can be a silver lining, and with practice, you will be able to face anything that comes your way.

Reflection

- How do I usually respond when I feel hurt?
- Where in my life am I assigning unnecessary weight or meaning to situations?
- How can I pause and choose a more empowering response to pain?

Affirmation

"I hold the power to choose how I respond to hurt."
"I release pain with wisdom and compassion, and I allow healing to flow through me."

Navigating the Ego

One of the greatest benefits of meditation is learning how to navigate the ego. As you become more aware of your inner world and learn to quiet the mind, life begins to feel clearer and more manageable. When you start to notice not only the constant mental chatter but also the stillness beneath it, you gain insight into how your mind truly operates. Once you can distinguish between noise of the ego and silence of your soul, you gain the ability to choose between them. With that choice comes the power to direct your thoughts and actions more consciously.

The ego is the voice that repeatedly moves into the foreground throughout the day. It constantly pulls you into reaction, judgment, anger, and drama. The ego anchors itself in these to stay alive. With regular meditation, this voice begins to lose its grip, allowing stillness to rise into awareness. That stillness opens the doorway to your higher self and helps you tune into the wisdom of the Universe. As you learn to access that guidance, you begin to trust it as a compass that gently leads you along your path.

I once had a coworker ask me what I thought the difference was between prayer and meditation. I told her that in prayer, you speak to God, and in meditation, God speaks to you. When you become quiet enough, you can actually hear what is being said.

The ego thrives on duality. Its dialogue creates an inner tug-of-war between opposing thoughts, like a mental ping-pong match. If you listen closely, your thoughts might sound familiar: "I'm going to be good and not eat that," followed shortly by, "One little piece won't hurt. I'll start again tomorrow." Most of us have experienced this internal debate. It is simply the ego attempting to maintain control by keeping us divided within ourselves.

Learning to work with the ego allows you to rise above perceived shortcomings and make conscious choices that lead you in a new direction. When you shift your thoughts, your actions begin to change, and different outcomes naturally follow. This is not about eliminating the ego, but about no longer allowing it to run the show.

In the early stages of my conscious communication with the Universe, I would often sneeze, so much so that it became a personal signal that I was aligned with what I was receiving. These days, the signals are quieter, a gentle tug behind my right ear, goosebumps, or a warm wave moving through my body. These sensations let me know that I am receiving or sharing messages in alignment with truth.

Before you can shift your thoughts, you have to be aware of them. Over time, I have learned to recognize different areas of awareness within myself. My ego tends to be most active in the left frontal region of my mind, while my higher self feels more present in the central right side. When I receive guidance from the Universe, I feel a subtle activation just behind my right ear. This awareness helps me discern which voice is speaking at any given moment. My ego has not disappeared, but I have learned to gently move it into the background when my higher voice is present.

Now it is your turn. I encourage you to set aside time each day not only to meditate, but also to become aware of which aspect of your consciousness is active. Pause a few times throughout your day and tune in how you're feeling and acting. Are you operating from ego and experiencing judgment, doubt, or inner conflict? You recognize this by feeling on edge, having difficulty relaxing or are hyper focused on a person or even. Or are you connected to your higher self, feeling peace, acceptance, love, and flow? You recognize this by feeling settled, calm, warm, hopeful, and positive. As you become familiar with your inner landscape, you will find it easier to shift your state of mind intentionally. That awareness can be deeply liberating. The mind will always wander, but peace and serenity require space. When you make room for silence, you reconnect with your natural state of being. In that stillness, you rediscover your innate power, the power to be yourself authentically, and to experience happiness from within.

When you notice yourself slipping into judgment or anger, toward yourself or others, pause. Take a deep breath. Center and choose a different perspective. This takes time and practice, but it is worth the effort. Over time, you may find yourself navigating life from a place of calm presence and quiet strength. The drama the ego feeds on loses its grip. You begin to recognize that you are already enough, and that peace lives in this recognition.

Take a chance on yourself and on humanity. Nothing is lost, but growth requires participation and forward movement. Each conscious step you take supports not only your own evolution, but that of the collective as well.

As Albert Einstein once said, "No problem can be solved from the same level of consciousness that created it." To move forward, we must first change how we perceive the challenges we encounter. Only then can meaningful transformation take place.

Accept the call to live with greater awareness and choose to carry the light through your words and actions. Move forward with trust and courage. As you learn to navigate away from your ego and align more fully with who you are meant to be, life opens in unexpected ways. In becoming yourself, you become a quiet force for change, creating ripples that extend far beyond you.

Reflection

1. When I feel inner tension, which voice is speaking, my ego or my higher self?
2. How does my body signal alignment with truth?
3. What daily practice helps me return to peace and stillness?
4. How can I create more space for silence in my life?
5. In what ways can I bring light and awareness into my everyday actions?

Affirmation

"I quiet my mind and open my heart."
"I am guided by peace, love, and higher wisdom."

Finding Your Power

Everyone carries an innate power, and that power expresses itself in distinctive ways. Some people communicate through eloquent words, others through creativity, and some through a quiet, steady presence. One expression is not better than another, at least not from a Universal perspective. What matters is becoming comfortable with your own unique way of being. Not everyone will resonate with your energy, and that is perfectly okay.

In today's world, especially with the constant noise of social media, certain voices appear louder than others. But volume does not equal power. In fact, there is often a great deal of noise and very little authentic truth. This is where discernment becomes essential. From a Universal perspective, we are all equal. When you use your power with pure intent, even if it touches only one person, you are living in alignment with your true essence.

To find your inner power, you must turn inward. Your power lives quietly within you, patiently waiting for your attention. This process takes time, honesty, and a willingness to release what you have been carrying. Meditation, sitting in silence and writing things out are all valuable methods to help with that. The good news is that once you reconnect with this inner strength, it becomes available to you whenever you need it. You begin to realize that you are the power and that your inner knowing, guidance, intuitive awareness, has always been there. The work lies in remembering and reclaiming it.

People often ask what personal power actually feels like. Many imagine it as confidence without fear, clarity without doubt, or strength without struggle. In truth, personal power is quieter and far more grounded than those ideas suggest.

You begin to recognize it when you no longer need constant reassurance from others. You still value connection and input, but you stop abandoning yourself in the process. Your decisions start coming from an inner steadiness rather than from urgency, fear, or the need to be validated.

You'll notice it in how you respond to life. Situations that once triggered you no longer pull you off center so easily. You pause before reacting. You choose your words with more care, not because you are suppressing yourself, but because you are no longer driven by the need to defend, explain, or prove who you are.

Personal power also shows up in your relationship with timing. You begin to trust your own pace. You stop forcing outcomes and allow things to unfold without losing faith in yourself. Even in moments of uncertainty, there is a quiet knowing that you will find your way through.

You may feel this shift in your body as well. There is less tension, less holding. Your breath deepens. Your posture softens yet becomes more grounded. You take up space more comfortably, without apology. You no longer shrink to keep others comfortable, nor do you feel the need to dominate in order to be seen.

Another clear sign is discernment. You become more selective with your energy. You recognize when a situation, relationship, or environment no longer aligns, and instead of guilt or self-doubt, you choose clarity. Walking away feels clean rather than dramatic.

Perhaps the strongest indicator of personal power is this: you begin to live from alignment instead of approval. You choose what feels true, even when it is uncomfortable. You speak honestly, guided by compassion rather than fear. You trust yourself enough to follow your inner guidance, even when the path ahead is not fully visible.

This is personal power. Not loud or forceful, but steady, embodied and rooted in deep self-trust.

If you have already begun this process, trust that you are exactly where you need to be. If not, start now. Take the first step and lay the foundation. There is no perfect moment. Ask the questions that lead you back to yourself. Discover what brings you joy and allow that to become your foundation.

Your inner voice does not need to be found. It needs to be trusted. You can strengthen your connection to your inner voice of truth and intuition by doing the following:

> 1. **Create moments of stillness;** Your intuition speaks quietly. Silence, slow breathing, or brief pauses throughout the day create space for inner guidance to surface.

> 2. **Listen to your body;** Your body signals truth before your mind does. Expansion, calm, or ease often indicate alignment, while tension or heaviness signal resistance.

> 3. **Notice the difference between intuition and fear;** Intuition feels steady and clear. Fear feels urgent, repetitive, and anxious. Learn to sense the difference before responding.

> 4. **Use writing to access clarity Journaling bypasses overthinking.** Write freely, without editing. Your inner voice often appears before logic steps in.

Your power is not something handed to you by circumstances, nor is it earned through outside approval or validation. It already belongs to you and when you access it, life begins to align. Even when you stumble, you know how to return to your center. That inner knowing is true power. From this place, you hold the key to your own fulfillment.

Once you reconnect with this energy, there is no need to force your way forward. When you move in alignment, doors open naturally and the right people appear. Obstacles begin to soften or fall away. Your energy is met by the Universe and is reflected back to you. You feel guided, supported, and free.

Reflection

1. What does personal power mean to me beyond material or external success?
2. In what areas of my life do I give my power away, and why?
3. In what areas of my life do I feel powerful and do I enjoy this power?
4. What limiting beliefs have I accepted as truth that no longer serve me?
5. Which suggested activities feel right for me for finding my inner voice and power?
6. What small daily action can help me live from my authentic, empowered self?
7. What is something I love to do and that makes me feel alive?

Affirmation

"My power is calm, steady, and infinite."
"I trust my inner wisdom and allow my light to guide the way."

Shadow Work

This chapter marks one of the most confronting and transformative parts of the journey, shadow work.

Shadow work is an invitation to turn inward and acknowledge the parts of yourself you may have kept hidden. It is the act of bringing awareness to what has long remained in the shadows. When you do this, you begin to create space for something new, healthier, and more aligned to take root in your life. While this process can feel uncomfortable or even frightening at times, it is profoundly freeing. Shadow work allows you to release what has been quietly holding you back.

Everyone has a shadow side within, hiding from our consciousness. We have hidden memories, feelings of shame, and beliefs that our flaws make us unworthy of love or belonging. To protect ourselves, we often wear masks, especially around those whose judgment we fear. Yet beneath that fear of judgment is something more painful, the fear of being unloved, unseen, or undeserving.

Shadow work asks for self-awareness, self-acceptance, and compassion. When something within us is triggered, we often respond from fear by lashing out, withdrawing, or shutting down. Over time, we build emotional walls to protect our most sensitive parts. Healing begins when we slowly and intentionally start to lower those walls.

While some aspects of shadow work can be done alone, support is sometimes necessary. On my own journey, I was guided by both a spiritual mentor and a licensed therapist, each playing an essential role in my healing. My trauma began at a very early age, and it took time, patience, and trust in the process to release it. Through this experience, I came to understand that asking for help is not a sign of weakness, but an act of strength.

Working with the shadow takes time. It requires courage to face buried emotions such as anger, resentment, and grief. These feelings may be uncomfortable, but they are part of the human experience. While they do not define who you are, they often shape how you respond to life. Many people become stuck here, identifying with the role of the victim without realizing that the door to freedom is already open. Sometimes, sharing the same painful stories brings a feeling of familiarity or validation, and that comfort can make letting go more difficult.

Facing your shadow means being honest with yourself. It means acknowledging your wounds and recognizing that healing is needed. We often create protective stories to avoid discomfort, but in this work, we gently begin to see beyond those narratives. As you notice the anger, resistance, and fear, you also begin to reclaim the power that has been hidden beneath them.

Acknowledgment is the first step. Without it, you are navigating in the dark. Once you recognize the story you have been telling yourself as simply a story, you gain the freedom to write a new one. This is where transformation begins. It requires commitment and consistency, but it is possible. The choice is yours, and the work, while challenging, is worth every step.

Forgive yourself for what you did not know. Begin again from a place of truth. Let this become your new foundation.

Move slowly and allow the transformation to settle before sharing it widely. In the early stages, confide only in those you trust deeply. Growth can be uncomfortable for others, especially when it challenges familiar dynamics. When your new way of being is still forming, outside opinions can unintentionally disrupt your momentum. Protect your energy until it feels stable and strong.

When you are ready, speak your truth. As you do, you may inspire others to begin their own healing. What a beautiful ripple that it creates, not only for you, but for all of us.

Reflection
- What part of myself have I been avoiding or judging?
- Can I identify a recurring emotional pattern that may be asking for healing?
- What would it look like to meet that part of myself with compassion rather than fear?

Take a few quiet moments to write freely, without judgment. Allow the words to flow as if your higher self is speaking gently to your shadow.

Affirmation

"I welcome all parts of myself with love and compassion."
"Through understanding my shadow, I reclaim my light."

Overcoming Loss

Life on this planet of duality inevitably brings both beauty and hardship. Moments of joy, such as marriage, the birth of children, or deep connection, exist alongside pain, loss, and struggle. The wheel of life keeps turning. Sometimes you find yourself at the top, sometimes at the bottom. Wherever you are, remember that life is always in motion.

When life becomes difficult, you may feel anxious, defeated, or broken. Painful experiences leave deep imprints. Grief, betrayal, fear, and despair can create emotional scars that take time to soften. Often, what hurts in the present stirs older wounds buried in the subconscious. In those moments, you are not only facing what is happening now, but also what has not yet been fully healed.

Pain can distort perception. It makes you question your worth, your direction, and sometimes even your faith. I know this place well, pleading for answers, feeling angry, wondering why. And yet, eventually, the storm does calm. The clouds begin to part, and light finds its way back in. Acceptance settles quietly. You begin to weave the experience into your life's story, allowing it to shape you rather than define you.

In the midst of hardship, it can help to step back and view your life from a higher perspective, like an eagle soaring above. From this vantage point, you remember the experience without being consumed by it. Distance creates clarity, and within that clarity, healing begins.

Some of our deepest pain comes through loss, especially the loss of someone we deeply loved. Grief has no timeline. It is not something we simply get over, but something we learn to live with and, eventually, honor. When someone dies, their physical presence may be gone, but their essence remains. Their energy weaves itself into who we are, quietly guiding us and reminding us of what matters.

There are souls whose presence shapes us at the core. My mother and my dear friend Grace were such souls for me. Their absence left a profound ache. Over time, that ache softened into something sacred. I carry my mother's resilience and wisdom within me, and Grace's light and laughter live on in my heart. Their teachings continue through me, shaping how I move through the world.

Loss teaches us to hold sorrow and beauty at the same time. It humbles us and opens us. It asks us to keep trusting life, even when it no longer makes sense. And when we are ready, it invites us to carry love forward in a new way, by becoming the light we once received from those we loved.

If you are grieving, allow yourself to feel it fully. Do not rush the process or try to numb the pain. Cry when you need to. Speak their name. Share their stories. Surround yourself with those who can sit with your grief without trying to fix it. Grief is not a problem to solve; it is an experience to be honored.

Here are some gentle ways to support yourself through loss:

- Create a simple ritual in their memory, lighting a candle, walking in nature, or sitting quietly with them in your thoughts.
- Write letters to the one you've lost. Say what was left unsaid. Express love, anger, gratitude, or longing.
- Keep something of theirs close, not as a shrine, but as a reminder that love does not end.
- Speak about them with those who knew them. Let their memory remain woven into your life.

- Ask yourself, how can I live in a way that honors them? What would they want for me now?

You may never stop missing them. Over time, grief becomes less of a weight and more of a companion. One day you realize you are living again, not because you have forgotten, but because you have integrated their presence into who you are.

They were part of your journey, and in a sacred way, they still are. Every step forward carries their legacy.

Growth happens when you choose to see challenges, even the loss of loved ones, as opportunities. These moments clarify what matters and reveal your inner strength.

Reflection

- What challenge in your life taught you the most about your own strength?
- How has grief, loss, or hardship reshaped the way you view love and connection?
- What lesson might your current challenge be asking you to learn?

Affirmation

"Even through pain, I grow stronger."
"I trust the flow of life and rise with every wave."

Forgiveness

Forgiveness is the act of releasing past hurt and the inner struggle that comes with it. It does not mean forgetting what happened, nor does it mean condoning harmful behavior. Forgiveness is about setting yourself free. When you let go of anger, resentment, and fear, you loosen the emotional ties that bind you to a person or situation that caused pain.

Holding on to unresolved emotions keeps you stuck. Over time, buried feelings can surface as physical illness, emotional imbalance, or a persistent sense of being trapped. Forgiveness interrupts that pattern. It allows healing to begin by restoring movement where energy has been held.

As Maya Angelou so clearly expressed, forgiveness is not about forgetting the past, but about releasing the hope that the past could have been different. What happened cannot be changed. What *can* be changed is how you carry your past forward.

We all carry the weight of our life experiences, some joyful, others deeply painful. While it may not feel like it in the moment, painful experiences often serve as catalysts for growth. disruption, we tend to remain in familiar patterns. Sometimes, it takes discomfort to move us forward.

After hardship, we are faced with a choice. We can remain tied to the story, identifying with the role of the victim and the familiarity it brings, or we can begin the healing process by choosing to let go.

Forgiveness does not erase the memory. It simply means the memory no longer holds power over your future.

Ask yourself honestly, who is being hurt by holding on? Often, the person who caused the pain has already moved on. They are no longer carrying weight, you are. Forgiveness is not for them. It is for you.

When forgiveness is chosen, energy begins to shift. Space opens for new experiences, new perspectives, and renewed vitality. By releasing what no longer serves you, you allow your mind and body to move forward with greater ease and clarity.

Especially now, as the collective energy feels more intense, forgiveness becomes essential. Life is already complex and demanding. Carrying unresolved pain only adds unnecessary weight. Forgive, not to minimize what happened, but to honor yourself. Release the past so it no longer defines you. Allow change to occur. Open the door gently and step forward when you are ready.

Reflection

- Who or what am I still holding on to that no longer deserves space in my heart?
- How might my life feel if I released that burden?

Take a few quiet moments to visualize yourself letting go. See the cords of resentment, pain, and attachment dissolving into light. Notice the peace that follows, and remember, forgiveness is not for them. It is for you.

Affirmation

"I release the past with love and gratitude."
"I forgive myself and others with ease and grace."
"My heart is free, and I open to the flow of peace and renewal."

Projection

Throughout your life, certain people will appear and act like mirrors. These mirrors reflect both your light and your shadow, often arriving at the exact moment you are ready to grow. Their presence may feel uncomfortable, triggering, or confusing, but their purpose is sacred. These "angels in disguise," as I like to call them, awaken you to truths you might not have been ready to see on your own.

Projection happens when someone stirs something inside you that you would rather avoid. Maybe they say something that hits a tender place, or their behavior highlights a pattern you haven't healed. The reaction is rarely pleasant. It can feel jarring, like stepping into a cold shower. However, these moments are invitations to evolve.

When you notice yourself becoming triggered, try to pause before reacting. Take a breath. Observe what emotion is surfacing, whether it is anger, fear, or sadness. Ask yourself what belief or memory may be activated. This moment of awareness is where choice returns. The less you define yourself by the words or actions of others, the more freedom you experience.

Think about the people who have triggered you the most. Chances are, many of them are no longer in your life. That's because once the lesson is integrated, the mirror is no longer necessary. When you shift, the vibrational match changes, and the dynamic either falls away or transforms naturally. Those who remain often continue to reflect on something meaningful back to you, something still asking for your attention.

These mirrors gently expose parts of yourself you may find uncomfortable, including shame, anger, insecurity, or fear. They shine light on old wounds you may have convinced yourself were already healed. If you recognize the pattern, relax into the emotion, and embrace the lesson. This is how growth happens. I've experienced this countless times. Some mirrors propelled me forward; others brought up deep wounds from my childhood that I thought I had already processed. I didn't always appreciate the discomfort then, but now I view these people as some of my greatest teachers.

Of course, we aren't just receivers of projection. We, int turn, act as mirrors, too. Sometimes we reflect on the truth others aren't ready to see. That reflection can be confronting, and some may react with anger, blame, or distancing themselves. While that can hurt, especially when you value the relationship, it's important to remember this isn't personal. It's part of their growth, just as your triggers are part of yours. If an interaction leaves you emotionally charged, replaying in your mind hours or even days later, pay attention. Something deep within you is asking to be seen. Try this process:

- Pause for a moment and simply notice your reaction.
- Take a slow, intentional breath.
- Acknowledge the emotion that's rising by asking, *what am I truly feeling right now?*
- Ask yourself what deeper wound this may be touching, is this tied to something from your past?
- Reflect on which part of you is asking for attention, compassion, or change; perhaps a place of old hurt, unspoken anger, fear of being seen, self-doubt, exhaustion, or a longing that has been ignored for too long.
- Decide if you're ready to take responsibility for your energy and shift it.
- Take one conscious step forward. Small, steady steps are more than enough to have a big impact.

Healing takes time. They say it takes at least 21 days to form a new pattern, and the Universe will often "test" your progress by sending another mirror your way. This isn't punishment; it's reinforcement, a way to help you solidify the new version of yourself you're becoming.

Projection is not something to fear. It is something to honor. These mirrors help you uncover who you truly are. They guide you back to your authentic self by showing you what still needs healing, what still requires attention, and what is already strong and beautiful within you.

While some mirrors bring discomfort, others bring clarity, joy, and encouragement. All of them, whether easy or challenging, are part of your growth.

Reflection

- Who in your life has recently acted as a mirror, showing you something about yourself?
- What emotional reactions are hardest for you to face, and what might they be trying to teach you?
- How can you practice compassion—for yourself and for those who trigger your growth?

Affirmation

"I welcome the mirrors in my life with gratitude. Every reflection helps me grow into a more conscious, loving version of myself."

Staying in the Moment

Each day, our minds move quickly from one thought to another, making it difficult to stay grounded and present. Even as we go about our daily routines, our inner dialogue often pulls us in multiple directions at once. This becomes especially challenging during difficult times, when the mind tends to spiral and create stress, anxiety, irritability, and even depression. In those moments, choosing presence becomes essential.

Most of us have experienced times when fear and uncertainty took over and our thoughts immediately jumped to the worst-case scenarios. When that happens, it takes intention to return to stillness. One simple and effective way to anchor ourselves is through our breath. Inhale slowly for a count of four, then exhale for a count of four. The exact count is not important, what matters is the steady rhythm. Our body responds naturally. Your heart rate slows. Tension eases. And you gently return to the present moment.

This simple practice prevents your thoughts from pulling us into the past or projecting into an imagined future. The truth is the only thing that truly exists is this moment. Everything else is a projection of the mind. Looking ahead often fuels anxiety, while looking back can stir regret. Neither place supports your growth. What we can control is how we respond to what is happening right now.

You always have a choice. You can respond with awareness, or you can get pulled into drama. Choosing awareness does not mean ignoring pain. It means allowing your emotions without becoming consumed by them. Drama keeps the mind spinning, replaying conversations and feeding the ego. Presence, on the other hand, brings calm, clarity, and peace.

The mind can only focus on one thing at a time. When you notice yourself spiraling, gently bring your attention back to your breath. Notice your surroundings. Feel your feet on the ground. Allow yourself to fully arrive where you are. With practice, this builds inner strength and allows you to move through difficulty with more grace.

I have experienced this firsthand. A few years ago, I had to consciously reset my thoughts, sometimes every fifteen minutes, just to stay grounded. I had been diagnosed with cancer, and around the same time, my husband lost his job. Fear took over. I worried about my health, my children, our finances, and the possibility of losing our home. My thoughts ran wild and they took me to dark places. Each time they did, I brought myself back to the present moment. I breathed deeply, sat quietly, and focused on what was real rather than the endless "what ifs." My mantra became "I will cross that bridge when it needs crossing", Over time, this practice became my refuge, a place of steadiness and peace.

If you are facing something difficult right now, do not lose faith. There is always a larger unfolding at work, even when you cannot yet see it. Breathe and trust that things will fall into place. Come back to the now, everything else can wait. With time, you may even find yourself drawn more to stillness than to chaos since you will have trained your mind to welcome this new state of mind.

Action always follows your thoughts. When you learn to guide your thoughts, you begin to make wiser choices. From those choices come greater clarity, strength, and peace.

Choose to be present in the now and do not see yourself as defeated. You have the ability to take the reins of your life in your hands and guide it forward, one conscious moment at a time.

Be here. Be now. Trust that from this space, anything is possible.

Reflection
- When was the last time I truly felt present?
- Which thoughts most often pull me out of the moment?
- How can I gently guide myself back when my mind begins to spiral?
- What small daily ritual could help me stay centered through-out the day?

Affirmation
"I am present, grounded, and peaceful."
"With each breath, I return to the beauty of this moment."
"In stillness, I find my strength."

Overcoming Your Fear

Most of our struggles begin in the mind and are rooted in fear. But here's a universal truth: the Universe only functions through love. I know this firsthand because of my encounter with a spirit at age twenty-seven, where I felt the overwhelming beauty of that love. That means concepts like fear, lack, and anger don't exist on the other side. However, here on Earth, we live in a world of duality, where fear is part of the journey. In healthy doses, fear serves as a protective mechanism, keeping us from harm. But when it becomes chronic or irrational, it turns into something paralyzing.

Fear is multi-dimensional. It can help us survive, but it can also keep us stuck. A healthy fear response might arise if you're walking alone at night and sense danger. That instinctive gut feeling is your body alerting you to stay cautious. That's fear serving its purpose.

Unhealthy fear, however, is different. It lives in your mind. It spins endless negative possibilities about what might happen and is not based in reality. It whispers that you're not good enough, that others will judge you, or that you'll fail if you try. This kind of fear is limiting, and restricts growth, expansion, and joy.

Learning to distinguish between healthy and unhealthy fear is essential. One lives in your gut, the other in your mind. Your gut sends real-time signals like tightness, nausea, or unease. These feelings are meant to be trusted. Your mind, on the other hand, fabricates stories and scenarios that haven't happened and likely never will. These thought patterns can feel real, but they are just that, thoughts, not truths.

We all experience moments of overthinking, self-doubt, and hesitation. But staying stuck in these loops prevents growth. If unchecked, they can lead to sadness, anxiety, depression, and even physical illness.

The key is awareness. Tune in to how your body responds in certain situations or around specific people. Listen to your gut and honor those signals. If you catch your thoughts spiraling into fear, pause, breathe, and shift your inner dialogue. This is not always easy but can be achieved. Focus your thoughts on something your hold dear, like a baby or beloved pet. This resets your awareness to love. You hold the power to change the story.

Instead of living from fear and being a prisoner of your thoughts, make the choice to use your power to change the story swirling in your mind. You have the power, Find that small spark of courage and nurture it. You can do this. Be consistent. With time and courage, your life will shift. Don't wait for permission, you don't need it.

Choosing to live from a place of love instead of fear is liberating. It opens your heart and makes you curious again. It reminds you that life is filled with possibilities, not threats. And it puts you back in the driver's seat of your own life.

Reflection

What fears are currently holding you back?

Take a moment to write them down and notice where in your body you feel them. Are they gut warnings or stories from your mind? Breathe into those spaces and visualize releasing the fear with each exhale.

Affirmation:

"I release fear and choose love. I trust my inner guidance and step forward with courage."

Choices

The ability to make conscious choices in the moment is one of the most powerful tools available to you. When you bring your awareness into the present, you begin to see situations more clearly, without the filters of past experiences or worries about the future. From this place of presence, you gain the ability to respond thoughtfully rather than react automatically.

Each of us has the capacity to quiet the mind. The real question is whether we follow negative thought patterns or choose to redirect them. When you notice yourself spiraling downward, pause. Take a few slow, intentional breaths. Gently guide your attention back to the here and now. Stay there as long as you can and when your thoughts drift again, simply bring them back, without judgment, to the now. The more often you practice this cycle of breath, awareness, and stillness, the stronger your inner compass becomes.

This is where you begin to reclaim your power, through the simple but profound act of choosing how you perceive the world and your place within it. When you learn to shift negative thoughts into more supportive ones, you realize that it takes the same amount of energy to think either way. With that awareness comes choice. Why not choose thoughts that uplift and support you?

Hardship is an inevitable part of life, without it, we would not learn and grow. What truly matters is how you respond when those challenges arise. Instead of allowing fear or stress to take over, anchor yourself in the present moment and respond from clarity. The past has already passed. The future has not yet arrived. The only place you can create change is right now.

Staying present takes effort, and like any skill, it strengthens with practice. It asks you to quiet the ego and tune into your higher self. Over time, the ego loosens its grip, and being present begins to feel more natural, even in the midst of difficulty. As you step out of drama and into awareness, something shifts. Peace replaces dread, stillness replaces chaos, and freedom replaces helplessness.

Make presence a daily practice, even if only for a few minutes at a time. Think of your mind as a muscle, the more you train it, the more responsive it becomes. You may find yourself thinking, "Things are fine right now, I don't need this." Yet it is precisely during calm moments that this practice becomes most valuable. When you train your mind while things are going well, it will support you when challenges arise. With time, this way of being becomes part of you. You begin to recognize that you can change your thoughts and actions at any moment. That realization alone is powerful.

Imagine living from a place where you set your own tone each day. Imagine responding instead of reacting, choosing clarity instead of confusion. You already have everything you need to do this, laying dormant within, all it needs is attention.

Take a breath. Notice where you are. Feel what is happening right now. Gently challenge yourself to remain in this awareness. Your choices are many, yet they can only be discovered when the mind is free from habitual patterns.

Choose consciously to be present. From this place, you are free to become who you are meant to be.

Reflection
- How often do I notice myself reacting instead of responding?
- Which situations tend to trigger automatic reactions for me?
- What might change if I paused and chose differently next time?

Take a few slow breaths and imagine responding with awareness rather than habit.

Affirmation
"I choose presence over distraction,
peace over chaos,
and love over fear."

Breathe

Breathe in,
Breathe out.

Breath is life. With every inhale, oxygen is delivered to every cell in our bodies. Without sufficient oxygen, our body cannot function optimally, our energy drops, our organs slow, and mental clarity fades. The beautiful truth is that we can shift our entire state of being with just a few conscious breaths.

Your breath changes everything. The choices you make from a relaxed, grounded state are very different from those made in stress or survival mode. When your body is nourished by oxygen, clarity returns. From this place, you respond with strength and calm rather than urgency or fear.

When we feel anxious or overwhelmed, we often hold our breath or breathe shallowly without realizing it. This unintentionally increases physical stress. In those moments, pause and turn inward and take four or five slow, steady breaths. As you inhale, imagine your breath filling your body, restoring, calming, and awakening your energy. With each exhale, feel tension soften and release. Let go of what no longer serves you. You don't need it for the direction you're heading.

Choose to breathe. Choose to soften. Choose to say yes to life as it is unfolding. You do not always need to hold on so tightly. Sometimes the most powerful thing you can do is to surrender and trust. Trust that the Universe has your back. Let go and let Source in and guide you to where you are meant to be.

Follow the natural rhythm of your breath. When you bring your attention to breathing, you anchor yourself in the present moment. The mind can only focus on one thing at a time, and in that moment, it is simply you and your breath. Of course, the mind will wander, that is natural. Each time it does, you have the opportunity to gently guide your awareness back. This simple act becomes a powerful way to ground yourself when life feels overwhelming.

Life will not always be gentle. It will send waves to test your footing, much like storms moving across the ocean. But when you return to your breath, center yourself, and respond with awareness, you learn to move with the current instead of fighting it. One choice empowers you; the other exhausts you.

Take a moment now. Sit comfortably. Close your eyes if that feels right. Let distractions fall away and bring your attention back to your breath. Inhale slowly and exhale with purpose.

Not everything in life needs to be difficult. Often, the smallest shifts bring the greatest change.

Just breathe.

Reflection

- When was the last time I truly paid attention to my breath?
- How does my body feel when I breathe slowly and deeply compared to when my breath is shallow or tight?

Affirmation

"With each breath, I return to peace, balance, and divine flow."

Reality

What is real? Do you know? Deep down, can you sense what holds true for you and what does not? Here is the paradox: very little in life is truly objective. Reality is shaped by the lens through which we experience the world. Two people can read the same sentence, witness the same event, or grow up in the same household and walk away with entirely different truths.

So, what changed? Not the facts, and not the words, but the filter through which each person interpreted their experience. Some people naturally approach life with optimism, while others focus on obstacles and challenges. Neither perspective is right or wrong, it is simply how reality is perceived.

Difficulties arise when we stop honoring the experiences of others and insist that our version is the only truth. Yet for every truth, there is another equally valid perception. This is part of being human.

I saw this clearly within my own family. A few years ago, my mom, my siblings, and I were sitting together, reminiscing about our childhood. Although we grew up in the same house, with the same parents, each of us shared completely different memories of how we were raised.

What made the difference?

It came down to how our parents related to each of us individually. My brother is male and the oldest child. I am the oldest daughter whereas my sister is the youngest. There is an eight-year gap between my brother and me, and an eleven-year gap between him and my sister. These differences shaped how our parents interacted with us, and those subtle distinctions formed very different inner worlds. It wasn't that our parents loved us more or less. They simply loved us differently.

I have seen this same principle play out in my own parenting journey, showing me how easily the mind can create a reality that feels completely true in the moment. There are only eleven months and twenty days between my daughters' birthdays. When I was pregnant with my youngest daughter, my greatest fear was that I would not be able to love her as deeply as I loved my first. My heart already felt so full loving my firstborn, and I could not imagine it stretching any further.

But the moment my youngest daughter was born, that fear dissolved completely. My heart expanded instantly. I loved her fully and still had endless love for both my older daughter and my husband. What had felt like an undeniable truth for months, and had created so much anxiety, turned out to be just a story, one rooted not in reality, but in uncertainty. And thankfully, it was proven wrong.

This is both the power and the trickiness of the mind. It can create a version of reality that feels entirely real, even when it is not. The good news is this: your mind is not your master. You can train it, just as you train your body.

One thought at a time.
One belief at a time.

You can shift your perception, and in doing so, transform your experience of reality. Begin to question what you believe to be true. Stay open and curious and allow your understanding to evolve. As it does, you naturally begin to live in alignment with who you truly are.

Reflection

Think of a time when you were convinced your version of an event was the absolute truth, only to later realize that someone else experienced it very differently.

- How did that realization make you feel?
- What does it reveal about how your beliefs shape your perception of reality?

Affirmation

"I honor my truth while allowing space for other perspectives."
"My mind is open, my heart is clear, and I trust reality to unfold through love and understanding."
"When I'm unsure about what is real, I take time to pause, breathe, and return to what feels steady and true within me."

Illusion

L ife is an illusion. That may sound like a bold statement, but bold does not mean untrue. The life you experience is largely shaped by your thoughts, your beliefs, and the stories you've told yourself over time. Most of us move through life without ever pausing to question those stories, accepting our thoughts as facts rather than possibilities.

Think back to your teenage years. Was your view of the world the same as it is now? Are your values, priorities, and beliefs unchanged? Of course not. You lived, learned, and evolved, and as you did, your perception of reality shifted as well.

So which version was real, the life you experienced then, or the one you are living now?

This is why life can be described as an illusion. It is fluid, constantly reshaped by perception and choice. At any given moment, you can turn left or right, and each direction creates a different experience, a different version of truth. The life you live is the one your mind constructs, and it always begins with your thoughts.

Each of us experiences life through our own lens. What feels right for one person may not feel right for another. It is your interpretation of events that shapes your reality. No one experience is more valid than another; it is all shaped by perception.

Take a moment to reflect on your own journey. Notice how your thought patterns and emotional responses have changed over time.

Some beliefs that once felt absolute, no longer hold power over you. Others may still quietly influence your choices. When you become aware of them, you are given a gift, the ability to choose what you carry forward and what you release.

This is where your power lives, in the conscious decision to let go of anything that keeps you from moving forward. With each shift in awareness, your perspective expands and you become more skilled at seeing patterns that may be impacting the reality you've been living within.

Change is constant. And within that movement, you are continually redefining your reality. So don't take life, or yourself, too seriously. Allow the illusion to guide you rather than confine you. Trust that every experience, every turn in the road, is shaping you, strengthening you, and inviting you to grow.

Have faith in the unfolding of your life. Trust that when support is needed, the right person will appear. And when you feel alone, remember your own resilience and know that you are never truly alone or unsupported. There is more out there working with you than you can see.

So, step forward, even when the path feels uncertain. Trust that what unfolds meets you where you are meant to grow. When you remember that you are co-creating the world you experience, reality softens and illusion loses its grip. From that place, life becomes less about control and more about awareness, presence, and allowing the journey to reveal itself, one moment at a time.

Reflection
- How has your perception of life shifted over the years?
- What stories or versions of yourself when you are young impacted you the most? Are those stories still relevant and true?
- Which beliefs once felt unquestionable but no longer define you?

- What illusions are ready to dissolve so you can live with more freedom and trust?

Affirmation
"I release the illusions that no longer serve me."
"I trust the flow of life and welcome change with faith, courage, and curiosity."
"Everything unfolds for my highest good."

Connection to Source

Our connection to Source is one of the most essential relationships we have. To disconnect from Source is, in many ways, to disconnect from ourselves. How can you truly know who you are if you deny a presence that already lives within you? You are created from the same essence as all of creation. Source is not separate from you, just as you are not separate from Source. At the deepest level, you are one.

Faith is the bridge that connects you to the Universe. It opens your awareness to a larger picture and to possibilities far greater than what the mind alone can grasp. When I speak of Source, I am not referring to a single image or definition. I am speaking of the Divine intelligence that exists in all things. Depending on where you are born, you may relate this to Christ, Buddha, Mohammed, Hindu traditions, or no formal religion at all. You may experience Source through the quiet intelligence of nature, the rhythm of the ocean, the stillness of a forest, or the feeling of deep inner knowing that arises when something simply feels true. Source can also be recognized in moments of love, compassion, creativity, and connection, when you sense that you are part of something far greater than yourself.

As you grow into the person you are meant to become, your connection to Source naturally deepens. Source is not something outside of you, it is the origin from which your inner guidance flows. Without this connection, it can be difficult to recognize your true self or understand your soul's purpose. When you look back over your life, you may begin to notice a quiet thread woven through every experience, moments of intuition, knowing, or gentle redirection that helped shape who you are today. That thread is your communication with Source. It rarely announces itself loudly. More often, it arrives as a whisper, a feeling, or an inner nudge. To hear it, you must become still enough to listen. Your inner guidance system is your direct line to the Universe, a constant dialogue that has been present all along, waiting for your attention.

Faith in a higher intelligence gently draws your attention inward. It awakens you to the universal presence already living within you. Intuition becomes your compass. The more you trust it, and trust yourself, the clearer your path becomes. Our purpose is to come as close as possible to fulfilling our soul's agreement while we are here.

With this awareness, you begin to sense the outcome of your actions before you take them, not only for your own benefit, but for the greater good as well. You come to understand that there are no true wrong turns, only experiences. Each one serves as a steppingstone, guiding you back to yourself.

We often label experiences as right or wrong, positive or negative. In truth, they are simply experiences, steppingstones along the way. Even moments that feel like missteps carry meaning. Painful experiences show you what no longer aligns with who you are, while joyful ones remind you of what your soul recognizes as home. In every experience, connection to a universal source is quietly taking place.

Move forward with confidence and an open heart. Let your intuition guide your decisions, it speaks more clearly than you may realize. Your soul often communicates through your body, especially through your gut.

When you learn to listen, its language becomes familiar:

- Warm, open, loving sensations are a gentle yes.
- Cold, tight, uneasy, or nauseating sensations are a clear no.

Many people move through life unaware of this inner compass.

They repeat patterns without realizing their soul is gently urging them toward a different path. As Einstein observed, doing the same thing repeatedly while expecting different results leads nowhere.

You can break the cycle, but it requires stillness and willingness. If something feels expansive and nourishing, you are likely aligned. If something feels heavy or off, take a moment to pause, reassess, and choose again. It does not have to be complicated.

The mind often overanalyzes and clouds decision-making. Your body, however, is honest. Listen to it. It is one of the most trustworthy connections we have to the wisdom within us. Trust its wisdom. Let it guide you forward.

Reflection

- Recall a moment in your life when perfect timing surprised you, when something fell into place just as you released control.
- How does your intuition feel when it says yes? How does it feel when it says no?
- What small daily practice could help you strengthen your connection to Source?

Affirmation

"I am one with the energy of the Universe."
"I trust my intuition to guide me with clarity and love."
"I listen to my body's message and trust that it is guiding me."

Division

As you move through life, you may feel pulled between two aspects of yourself: your physical self, often driven by ego, and your spiritual self, guided by higher awareness. We've all felt this inner tug-of-war, much like the familiar image of the angel on one shoulder and the devil on the other, each pulling you in a different direction.

But here's the truth: you can shift between them at any moment.

In every interaction and every decision, you get to choose which voice to follow, the ego or your higher self. This is your life, and you hold the reins. You can change direction at any time; that is your innate power.

When you live primarily from the physical realm and are rooted in ego, life is often filtered through fear, competition, or the need for control. In this state, empathy diminishes and intuition grows quiet. Your world becomes limited to what you can see or touch, and your ability to look beyond self-imposed boundaries is reduced.

On the other hand, if you live only in the spiritual realm, you may feel disconnected from the practical aspects of life. Your inner world may feel rich and expansive, yet grounding, structure, and common sense can fall away. Daily responsibilities like work, finances, and stability may begin to feel overwhelming.

You've likely encountered people who lean heavily into ego, driven by control, fear, or a lack of compassion. And you may also know those who live almost entirely in spirit, so ungrounded that they drift through life without direction or stability. Neither extreme is sustainable.

The magic lives in the middle.

The goal is balance. Neither extreme supports long-term growth. Life is meant to be lived fully, both in the physical and the spiritual. You are here to learn, to grow, and to fulfill the soul agreement you made before entering this lifetime. Yes, you chose to be here, and yes, you chose the lessons you wanted to explore. Let that settle for a moment.

As you learn to walk the line between ego and spirit, practices like meditation, breathwork, or simple moments of stillness help you access that quieter wisdom. Even a few conscious breaths can bring you back to center.

Over time, you learn to pause, breathe, and choose consciously. You begin to feel the difference between reacting from habit and responding with awareness. With practice, this becomes second nature.

That is the invitation: to nourish the voice of love rather than fear, to choose balance over chaos, and stillness over noise.

In that rhythm and flow, you find your strength. You walk with greater ease. You become the bridge between your human self and your highest self, the one who chooses love again and again, and in doing so, you come home to yourself.

Reflection

- Think of a moment when you reacted from fear or ego. How might that moment have felt different if you had paused and listened to your higher self?
- What helps you return to balance when life feels like a tug-of-war between your human and spiritual sides?
- How can you honor both your practical needs and your soul's calling today?

Affirmation
"I am both human and divine."
"I walk in balance between body, mind, and spirit."
"With each moment, I choose love over fear and harmony over chaos."

From Anger to Awareness

Anger is often the emotion we notice first, but it is rarely the whole story. More often than not, anger is a surface response, a signal pointing toward something deeper that has not yet been acknowledged. Beneath anger usually live emotions such as hurt, fear, grief, or disappointment. Some of these emotions originate in the past, while others arise through everyday interactions in the present. At some point in life, everyone carries unresolved emotions. When they remain unseen or unexpressed, they often transform into anger, not because we are failing, but because we have not yet learned how to listen beneath the surface.

Anger can feel powerful and immediate, but it rarely leads to true resolution. It reacts rather than reveals. When anger arises, pause and ask yourself, *"What am I really angry about?"* Most of the time, the person or situation in front of you is not the true source. They are merely the catalyst, a mirror bringing a deeper emotion to the surface so it can finally be seen. The solution does not exist outside of you. It lives within.

Healing takes time, honesty, and courage. Often, we unknowingly stand in our own way and, at times, even sabotage our progress. Expectations, especially the ones we place upon ourselves, are a common source of anger. When it surfaces, ask yourself whether your expectations were realistic, or whether you were unconsciously trying to fill an unmet need through another person or situation.

Many people are unaware of the true roots of their anger. We react without pausing to understand why. Yet the truth is, no one else *makes* us angry. We choose how we respond, consciously or unconsciously, and we are ultimately responsible for our reactions. Awareness begins the moment we stop looking outward for answers and gently turn inward instead.

Unresolved emotions do not simply disappear when ignored. Over time, they settle into the body and express themselves through tension, discomfort, or dis-ease. I often witness this during my private Reiki sessions. Clients may arrive with back pain, stomach issues, or tightness in their shoulders. From energetic perspective, these symptoms frequently reflect unprocessed emotional patterns. Everything is energy. When energy becomes stuck and remains so for too long, it seeks expression through the body. Left unattended, this imbalance can develop into chronic issues.

Emotions may also show up differently depending on how the body holds energetic tension. In women, unresolved anger often settles in the stomach and heart areas and may move into the throat, reflecting imbalance in the solar plexus, heart, and throat centers. In men, anger frequently concentrates in the lower abdomen or pelvic region, often presenting as inflammation, lower back discomfort, or challenges related to grounding and vitality. Any blockage within the body interferes with its natural flow, which is why reflection and energetic rebalancing are so important.

This work invites you to slow down and meet your emotions honestly. When anger surfaces, pause and turn inward. Ask yourself the difficult questions. *"What am I really feeling? What part of me feels unseen, hurt, or afraid?"* As you begin to address the deeper layers beneath anger, you may notice how much lighter both your body and mind start to feel. Releasing stored emotion creates space, not only for healing, but for renewed clarity, vitality, and freedom.

Loving yourself means allowing yourself to feel fully, without judgment. Holding onto anger does not protect you. It keeps you tied to the very experience you wish to move beyond. Awareness offers another path, one rooted in compassion rather than suppression. When awareness replaces reaction, anger softens and understanding begins to grow.

I learned this lesson deeply through my own experience after my mother passed away. In the weeks following her death, I believed I was managing well. I told myself I was strong and able to move forward without difficulty. Yet my mother came through with a message, asking me to be mindful of my heart. At the time, I did not fully understand what she meant. Days later, during a Reiki session with a trusted friend, I received the same message, even though I had not shared my earlier experience with anyone.

As she worked with me, I became aware of how tightly my heart was holding on. Beneath the surface, I was afraid that letting go would mean forgetting my mother or losing her presence. Once I recognized that this fear was unfounded, that love does not disappear through release, something shifted. I let go, and my heart felt instantly lighter. Had I ignored that awareness, the emotional weight might have settled into my body over time. Instead, I chose to listen.

Do not skip this step in your own journey. We all experience emotions. How we meet them determines whether they become a source of suffering or a doorway to healing. Anger, when met with awareness, becomes information rather than a weapon. Beneath it lies the key to your freedom. When you are willing to move below the surface, uncover the truth it guards, and respond with compassion, you reclaim your power.

This is not about forcing yourself to feel better. It is about listening more deeply. When you honor what is truly present within you, anger no longer controls you. It transforms. Understanding replaces resistance. Healing becomes possible. And with that healing comes peace, clarity, and the freedom to move forward with an open heart.

Reflection
- Think of a recent moment when anger surfaced.
- What emotion may have been underneath it, hurt, fear, grief, or disappointment?
- Where do you feel this emotion in your body, and what might that area be asking for?
- Write down one gentle way you can express or release this emotion with awareness and care.

Affirmation
"I meet my emotions with honesty and compassion."
"Through awareness, I release anger and create space for healing, peace, and freedom."

Standing in Your Own Strength

Standing in your own strength is not about force or authority. It is about returning to yourself again and again. It is the quiet confidence that grows when you trust your inner compass and allow it to shape your choices. Strength shows up when you no longer shrink to keep the peace, when you pause instead of reacting, and when you choose alignment over expectation. It is steady, grounded, and deeply personal. It does not demand recognition or approval from the outside world. It has always lived within you, waiting not to be proven, but to be embodied.

For a long time, I misunderstood strength. I believed it meant holding everything together, staying agreeable, and avoiding conflict. I thought being strong required endurance and silence. Over time, I came to understand that true strength often looks much quieter. It shows up in calm honesty, even when your voice feels uncertain. It appears when you step back instead of explaining yourself again and again. It lives in the choice not to engage in dynamics that drain you, even when that choice feels uncomfortable at first.

One of the clearest ways that strength began to show up in my life was through boundaries, not dramatic ones, but honest ones. I stopped overextending myself to keep others comfortable. I began listening to the signals in my body, the tightness in my chest, the fatigue in my shoulders, the subtle resistance when something did not feel right, and I honored those cues instead of pushing past them. Each time I chose to pause, to say no, or to take space without guilt, something shifted. I felt more rooted, more present, and more aligned with myself. This is strength in action, not loud or forceful, but steady and self-respecting.

Strength also reveals itself through emotional awareness. When something triggers you, it is easy to blame the other person or the situation. But strength asks a deeper question: *"What part of me is being activated? What belief is being touched?"* Instead of reacting immediately, strength invites reflection. It creates a small but powerful space between stimulus and response. In that space, you reclaim your choice. You respond consciously rather than automatically.

This strength is not given to you by others. It is not defined by your upbringing, your culture, or your past achievements. It does not depend on validation or approval. It grows each time you choose honesty over appeasement, clarity over confusion, and self-trust over self-doubt.

When you stand in your own strength, your world begins to shift. You become less shaken by other people's opinions and less compelled to prove yourself. You invest your energy more intentionally. You begin to notice where you are aligned and where you are compromising yourself. And when you find yourself of course, as we all do at times, you know how to return. You pause. You realign. You listen inward and adjust.

Standing in your own strength does not mean you never feel fear or uncertainty. It means you move forward despite them. It means you trust yourself to meet whatever arises. The strength you are searching for has always been within you. It is your truth, your inner compass, your steady foundation. The more you return to it, the more natural you live from it.

You already carry this strength. All that remains is your willingness to stand in it.

Reflection

- When do I feel most grounded and steady within myself, even without external validation?
- In what situations do I tend to shrink, overexplain, or abandon my own needs to keep the peace?
- What signals does my body give me when I am out of alignment, and how do I usually respond to them?
- Identify one small moment today where you can pause, listen inward, and choose alignment over expectation.

Affirmation

"I stand firmly in my own strength."
"I trust my inner compass and honor what feels true for me."
"With calm confidence and self-respect, I choose alignment, clarity, and steadiness in who I am becoming."

Nurture

Nurturing the soul means creating space to step away from the noise of the world and return to yourself. It is an intentional pause, a softening, a willingness to sit with your own thoughts and feelings without distraction. Solitude becomes sacred when you allow it to be, because in that quiet space, your inner voice can finally rise above the constant demands of daily life.

In moments of stillness, when you are alone and fully present, your truth begins to speak. It may not always tell you what you want to hear, but it will gently guide you toward what you need. Presence nurtures because it restores your connection to yourself. When you are present, you are no longer pulled into yesterday's regrets or tomorrow's worries. You are anchored in the now, and in that anchoring, your nervous system begins to settle. Your body softens. Your intuition becomes easier to recognize.

Nurturing your soul does not require grand gestures. It often lives in the small, consistent acts of care. It may look like sitting quietly with your morning tea before the house awakens, taking a walk without your phone, journaling honestly about what you are feeling, saying no when your body feels tired, turning off the news or stepping outside to feel the sun on your face or the air against your skin. These simple choices signal to your inner world that you are listening.

When you consistently make space for yourself, trust begins to grow. You start to recognize the subtle difference between fear and intuition. Fear feels urgent, loud, and pressured. Intuition feels calm, steady, and clear, even when it invites you to make a difficult decision. The more you nurture yourself, the more familiar that quiet guidance becomes.

Nurturing your soul also means honoring your free will. Each time you choose to listen inward rather than follow external expectations, you strengthen your relationship with yourself. You begin to recognize that you always have a choice, to live according to inherited rules and unspoken obligations, or to honor what feels true for you. Stepping away from the familiar takes courage, especially when cultural or familial conditioning has shaped your decisions for years. But nurturing yourself creates the inner safety needed to make those choices consciously.

As you deepen this practice, freedom naturally follows. Freedom to think your own thoughts rather than repeat beliefs that no longer fit. Freedom to follow your heart instead of shrinking for approval. Freedom to expand instead of stagnating. Like an eagle rising above the landscape below, you gain perspective when you trust your inner guidance. One path leads to growth and vitality, the other to quiet resentment or regret. Nurturing helps you recognize the difference.

If the answers that arise within you feel challenging but calm at their core, trust them. True growth may stretch you, but it does not create the sharp, anxious warning your body gives when something is wrong. The Universe does not abandon you. It gently nudges, again and again, until you are ready to listen. Nurturing is not about escaping life. It is about strengthening your connection to yourself so that when you engage with the world, you do so grounded, clear, and aligned.

When you choose yourself with honesty and care, you are not selfish. You are honoring your soul's quiet request to be seen. Your soul is not asking for perfection. It is simply waiting for your attention.

Reflection
- Where in your life are you still following others' expectations instead of your own truth?
- What small act of self-nurturing could you offer yourself today to realign with your soul's calling?
- Sit quietly and listen, your heart already knows the answer.

Affirmation

"I nurture my soul with love and presence."
"I honor my truth, trust my intuition, and give myself permission to soar."

Soul Intermissions

Soul intermissions are the intentional pauses you take to reflect on your life. Without these meaningful breaks, it is easy to slip into autopilot, moving from one moment to the next without awareness. We live in a world filled with noise, distraction, and constant demands. In that pace, you move from one task to another, one obligation to the next, rarely stopping to examine where you are headed.

You begin connecting the dots unconsciously, progressing from step one to step two, from step two to step three, until something or someone suddenly interrupts your momentum. Only then do the deeper questions rise to the surface:

What do I truly want?

Am I fulfilled?

Is this path aligned with who I am becoming?

If you do not give yourself intentional time to reflect on your current course, to check in with your thoughts, emotions, and overall well-being, you may eventually arrive at a place you no longer recognize or like. When you never pause to ask, *"Does this work for me? Do I feel aligned? Is this still my path? What needs adjusting?"* you risk slowly losing your way. Research shows that approximately 35–55 percent of Americans experience burnout at levels that interfere with functioning at their fullest capacity. Burnout and chronic stress often manifest outwardly as checked-out behavior, short tempers, impatience, cancelled plans, loss of interest in activities that once brought joy, and increasing isolation. I lived through all of these symptoms over the years, driven by the demands of family and work, while neglecting my own emotional needs and consistently putting myself last. Over time, this led to feeling completely lost and forgetting who I truly was.

Without regular soul intermissions, your well-being can slowly begin to erode. Over time, this imbalance may show up as dis-ease in the body, mind, or spirit. When that happens, the Universe, or Source, may step in, not as punishment, but as a loving interruption. It's an invitation to pause, reflect, and redirect. Just as the sun always reappears after the darkest storm, peace returns once you honor what your body, mind, and soul have been quietly asking for. Taking these pauses requires courage, because they ask for honesty with yourself.

We are never truly stuck. We have free will, and we can always change direction. But rather than waiting for the Universe to force us to slow down, we can choose to take these soul pauses now. We can begin simply by tuning into your body for five minutes at the start of your day. Gently scan your physical, emotional, and spiritual state and ask, *"What needs my attention today?"* Even if we can't tend to it immediately, acknowledge it and return to it later. What matters is that we listen.

Give yourself permission to pause in whatever way feels nourishing to you. For some, it may be a quiet walk along the beach or a hike through nature. For others, it could be journaling, time at a spa, or simply sitting in meditation. The form itself is not what matters. What matters is the intention behind it, choosing to spend meaningful, uninterrupted time with yourself.

Recently, I drove up to one of my favorite spots in the mountains and sat quietly on a warm rock in the sun, feeling the breeze move around me. There was nothing to accomplish, nowhere to be. In that stillness, I felt my thoughts settle. The tension from work softened. I could breathe again. Moments like that allow space for reflection, for releasing stress, and for gently reconnecting with yourself.

Another simple practice is listening to soft music and allowing your body to relax while your thoughts move freely, without judgment or the need to fix anything. Sometimes the greatest clarity comes not from effort, but from stillness.

Ignoring your well-being does far more harm than good, especially over time. Presence is preventative. Learn to read your body's signals and respond with care. Avoidance may feel easier in the moment, but it often leads to deeper imbalance later. This is not meant as a warning rooted in fear, but as an invitation to reclaim your power. Being proactive strengthens you; being reactive drains you. One restores balance, the other depletes it. Choose wisely.

When you approach these moments of reflection with grace, the Universe responds in kind. Life begins to flow more smoothly. Answers arrive without force. And before long, you find yourself realigned, living from a place of clarity, balance, and authenticity, back on the path you were always meant to walk.

Reflection

- When was the last time you gave yourself true permission to pause?
- What is your body or heart quietly trying to tell you right now?
- How can you create regular soul intermissions before life creates one for you?

Affirmation

"I honor my need to pause and reflect".
"Each moment of stillness reconnects me with my truth and restores my balance."

Letting Go

Letting go is one of the most important, and one of the most difficult, lessons you will encounter in life. It is not easy, but it is essential if you wish to heal, grow, and become the best version of yourself. Holding on to past trauma, emotions, or old stories keeps you anchored to your past and prevents you from fully living in the present.

Most people do not realize they are holding onto something until it begins to show up in their body, their reactions, or their relationships The first step is awareness. Identify what it is you are holding on to. You may consciously desire abundance, love, or success, yet unknowingly sabotage yourself because something within you remains unhealed. Once you can name the emotion, belief, or memory that is still active, you can begin to consciously interrupt the old pattern and choose differently.

Each day, take a quiet moment to go inward and ask yourself where your energy feels stuck. When you identify it, gently begin the work of releasing it. Don't rush the process. It will take as long as it needs to. What matters is that you begin, and that you stay committed.

This is how real change happens.

This is how healing unfolds.

This is how you come home to yourself.

Your ego will not welcome this process. It thrives on familiarity and resists change, even when that familiarity is painful. The ego helped shape the identity you've lived from, so when you begin to shift your thinking, it will push back. The deeper the wound or the more ingrained the belief, the stronger the resistance may feel. Still, with persistence and compassion, you can move through it.

Science suggests it takes at least twenty-one days to establish a new habit. During this time, awareness is key. Each time your mind drifts back toward an old story, gently bring it back to the present moment. Your breath is a powerful ally here, slow, steady, and conscious breathing helps regulate both the mind and the nervous system.

If your past holds deep hurt, such as physical or sexual abuse, the imprint may live not only in your memories but also within your body. Trauma does not simply disappear with time. It can settle into the nervous system, into the muscles, into the quiet spaces within you. In these cases, healing becomes a gentle, twofold journey, tending to both the mind and the body with patience and compassion.

Support can be a sacred part of this process. Working with a trauma-informed therapist or guide can help you safely untangle painful memories, so they no longer feel as though they are happening in the present. At the same time, body-centered practices such as mindful movement, breathwork, grounding in nature, or simply placing a hand over your heart and breathing slowly can begin to restore a sense of safety within. The goal is not to force release, but to gradually remind your body that it is no longer in danger.

As you continue this work, it does become easier. Moving through discomfort creates space. You may notice a lightness returning, a subtle shift in how you see yourself and the world. Healing from deep trauma also involves reclaiming your sense of self. This may mean learning to set boundaries, allowing safe relationships to support you, or slowly reconnecting with your body in ways that feel empowering rather than overwhelming. Each small act of self-trust becomes a step toward wholeness.

Letting go often brings us face to face with forgiveness, not as an obligation, but as a quiet invitation. Forgiveness is not about excusing what happened or pretending it did not matter. It is about loosening the emotional hold that keeps you bound to experiences that have already run their course. This includes forgiving others, and just as importantly, forgiving yourself. When the past remains tightly held, it continues to shape present thoughts, reactions, and choices, often without conscious awareness. In the same way, the need for control can feel protective, especially after hurt or disappointment. Yet control keeps the heart guarded and the body braced. Letting go asks for something gentler, a willingness to trust that life unfolds within a larger rhythm than the one we try to manage. You may not see the entire path ahead, but you can choose to release your grip on what has already been lived. In that release, something begins to shift. The mind clears, the body softens, and space opens where heaviness once settled. Fresh energy, new insight, and unexpected possibilities find their way in. Letting go is not about losing something, it is about creating room for who you are becoming.

As you begin to loosen your grip, something shifts. The mind quiets. The body softens. Space opens where heaviness once lived. New energy is able to move in, bringing clarity, insight, and possibility. What once felt constricted begins to expand. Letting go is not an ending, it is a return. A return to yourself, to your inner wisdom, and to a life that has room to breathe again.

Reflection

- What am I holding on to that no longer serves me?
- Where do I feel this energy in my body?
- What am I afraid might happen if I truly let go?
- What would freedom feel like if I released this completely?
- What small step can I take today to begin that release?

Affirmation

"I release the past with love and gratitude."
"I trust that letting go creates space for new blessings to enter my life."
"I surrender control and allow the Universe to guide me with grace."
"I am free. I am light. I am whole."

The Self

To live in truth with who you are, you must take time to get to know yourself. This requires stepping away from the noise of daily life and honestly reassessing your thoughts, emotions, actions, relationships, and goals. Without this pause, it becomes easy to drift, living on autopilot rather than with intention.

As you mature, you change. What once felt important may no longer hold importance. Through reflection and re-evaluation, you create space to make meaningful adjustments. Change does not need to be announced or justified. It is a sacred process between you and the Higher Source you feel connected to, whether you call that God, the Universe, or something else entirely.

In moments of reflection, you may discover areas of your life that feel out of alignment. You might notice that certain habits, relationships, or ways of living no longer reflect who you are becoming. Or you may find that you feel content and aligned right where you are. Either outcome is valuable. Regular self-check-ins allow you to consciously choose whether to remain where you are or begin again. You are the creator of your life, and each choice shapes its direction.

If you feel dissatisfied or uncertain, turn inward to locate the source of that friction. Once you identify it, take gentle action. Begin by stepping away from unnecessary noise and drama. While the world often equates progress with constant motion, clarity is most often found in stillness. Slow down. Breathe. Take a walk. Sit in quiet. In solitude, answers emerge and clarity takes shape.

If daily solitude feels unrealistic, even fifteen minutes of intentional stillness can make a difference. Meditation, reflection, or quiet breathing creates space for insight. Without these moments, emotional stagnation, chronic stress, and what I call *Universal blindness* can develop, a loss of direction, perspective, and connection. When you create space, you invite in fresh energy, new thoughts, and inspired action.

When this inner shift is held in a private sanctuary, it carries greater depth. Think of it as a quiet agreement between you and the Universe, honored through small, consistent steps. When change is rushed or exposed too quickly, it can lose its grounding, and you may find yourself returning to old patterns. True transformation takes time.

Ultimately, you have free will. You can remain where you are, or you can choose to step beyond what feels familiar. One path offers comfort and certainty, the other invites growth and expansion.

Choosing growth may feel uncomfortable at first, and at times even painful. Yet expansion asks for openness, a willingness to move beyond what you have known. Universal wisdom is always available to you, but it reveals itself only when you quiet the noise and allow yourself to listen.

We live our lives twice: once through experience and once through reflection. When you look back on your life, what do you want to see, peace or regret? Let the choices you make today shape the memory you will one day reflect upon. Choose the self you create with awareness. Choose with care.

Reflection

- When was the last time I truly paused to listen to my inner voice?
- Which parts of my life feel aligned, and which feel out of harmony?

- What am I avoiding that my soul is asking me to face?
- How can I create space for stillness and self-reflection in my daily life?
- What small change could I make today that would honor who I am becoming?

Affirmation

"I honor the sacred relationship I have with myself."
"Through reflection and stillness, I discover my truth."
"I choose growth, authenticity, and peace."
"I am aligned with the wisdom of my Higher Self."

Soul Direction

Soul direction is about orientation. It is the conscious act of realigning yourself with the path that feels true to who you are becoming. When you listen to your inner voice, your intuition, you begin to sense where your life is asking for adjustment. This is not about comfort or care; it is about clarity. It is about choosing your course with awareness.

Many of us move through life from one obligation to the next without pausing to reflect. We operate on autopilot, responding to expectations, responsibilities, and external demands. Over time, this can create a subtle drift away from our selves. Not because we intend to lose our way, but because we rarely stop to ask whether the direction we are heading still feels aligned.

Soul direction asks you to slow down long enough to notice.

It invites honest self-inquiry, without judgment or criticism. It requires courage to look at your life as it is and ask whether your choices reflect what you truly value.

You might begin with questions such as:

- What am I creating in my life right now?
- What do I genuinely want?
- Do my current choices reflect who I am becoming?
- Do I feel fulfilled?
- Does the life I am living bring me meaning and joy?
- Why do I give more weight to others' opinions than to my own inner knowing?

- What keeps me from trusting myself fully?
- Where might I be holding myself back?
- What small adjustment can I make today?

These questions are not meant to overwhelm you or demand immediate answers. They are meant to gently illuminate your path. Even the willingness to ask them shifts something within you. Awareness creates direction. And direction, once clarified, allows you to move forward with intention rather than habit.

To find your soul's direction, you must make space for solitude and reflection. Breathe. Become still. Be honest with yourself. Reflection invites clarity, and clarity reveals truth. That truth may not always be comfortable, and you may not be ready to act on it immediately, and that's okay. Truth does not disappear when ignored. It waits patiently. And if you try to run from it, the Universe has a way of gently guiding you back when the time is right.

The wisest choice you can make is to honor yourself. Follow your own truth and your own joy. The alternative is to live in the shadow of expectations placed upon you by parents, culture, or society. Many people spend their entire lives there, never stepping fully into who they are meant to be. But you are not meant to live small or hidden. You have every right to live according to your own design.

True fulfillment and soul expansion do not happen by accident. They require reflection, honesty, and a willingness to change, not only in how you think, but in how you live each day. Choose to live a life that is authentic, aligned, and unapologetically yours.

Reflection

- What does nurturing my soul look like in my daily life?
- When do I feel most connected to my inner truth?
- Whose expectations am I still trying to meet?
- What would change if I fully trusted my intuition?
- What simple act of self-care can I begin today to honor who I am becoming?

Affirmation

"I listen to my soul and trust its wisdom."
"I honor my truth and follow my inner guidance."
"I release the need to please others and choose authenticity."
"I honor my being with love, patience, and compassion."

$\mathcal{L}$ove

$\mathcal{L}$ove is the most beautiful and expansive emotion we can experience here on Earth. All of us are connected to the Divine, even if we are not always aware of that connection. We are created from the same essence as Source, and at our core, we are infinite, loving beings. When you truly accept this, it becomes easier to see people and life itself through the lens of love. Your natural state is one of compassion, truth, and light. When you filter your experiences through that awareness, you begin to see beauty not only in what is, but in what can become.

What is love? Who is it meant for? How do we receive more of it? Why don't I feel loved? Consciously and unconsciously, we ask ourselves these questions again and again. Love cannot be seen or touched, yet it is deeply felt. Love is energy, moving from one soul to another. Most importantly, it is something we are capable of both giving and receiving. We are enough, we are worthy, powerful, and absolutely deserving of love.

I was blessed to experience this Divine love firsthand at the age of twenty-seven, during an encounter with an angelic being. Words cannot fully capture the intensity or purity of that moment. I felt completely surrounded by love, a love so vast, peaceful, and profound that it went beyond anything the mind can comprehend. To this day, I can recall every detail and sensation of that experience. While I have felt love many times since, nothing has ever come close to the depth and serenity of that encounter. Divine love is gentle yet immensely powerful, and our human bodies can only partially hold it.

As adults, this natural state of love often surfaces instinctively when someone is hurt, grieving, or afraid. Unless empathy has been deeply wounded, we respond with compassion in these moments. This response is innate. Children as young as two will show affection or concern when someone is unwell. They instinctively want to help. Our pets do the same, sensing when we are upset and offering comfort without words. Love is our default setting.

You are love. That is the frequency you originate from, a loving Universe. Through love, we empathize, connect, and heal. Even plants respond to loving energy. Dr. Masaru Emoto demonstrated that words and intention influence the molecular structure of water. Since our bodies are largely made of water, this reminds us how important it is to be mindful of the energy we surround ourselves with and direct toward ourselves.

Over time, life experiences can distort our perception of love. Influences such as family, relationships, work, and culture can create limitations around how we give and receive love. It can feel as though a fog settles in, making it harder to see love clearly. When we restrict love, especially self-love, we begin to doubt our worth. This disconnection can lead to low energy, isolation, and even depression.

Consider a newborn baby. A baby enters the world untouched by conditioning, responding with wonder, curiosity, and openness. When surrounded by love, a child feels safe to explore and grow into a confident, compassionate being. When met with anger, neglect, or emotional absence, the child retreats, becoming anxious or fearful. Children mirror their environment, and those early impressions influence their thoughts, emotions, and even their cells. A lack of love creates stress, and prolonged stress can eventually manifest as illness.

Love leaves you in a state of contentment, a quiet inner knowing that you are enough. Through love, you can accept others for who they are, rather than who you believe they should be. True love is eternal. It surrounds us constantly, if we are willing to see it. When you accept love, love meets you where you are.

So why do we struggle with love? Often, it is fear of rejection. Somewhere deep inside, we may believe we are not good enough, that something is wrong with us, or that we do not deserve love. These beliefs are not truth, they are illusions.

Over time, we absorb messages from others telling us we don't measure up, that we are too much or not enough. Eventually, we begin to believe them and, often unknowingly, pass them on to others. This is where awareness must step in.

The Universe is made of love. We are love. Everything else is distortion. The ego thrives on fear, drama, and separation. It needs these to survive. Your Higher Self, however, operates solely from love. It forgives, accepts, and exists in peace, which is truth.

Begin by looking at yourself with kindness. Stand in front of the mirror and gently overwrite old beliefs. Tell yourself you are lovable. Tell yourself you are enough. Tell yourself you are perfectly created from Divine essence. This is not arrogance, it is truth. Each day, replace self-criticism with compassion. This is how you begin to open the door to self-love and allow love to flow freely into your life.

Ultimately, the choice is yours. You can remain where you are, or you can choose love. The outcomes are very different. Love will always guide you home.

Reflection
- How do I express love toward myself each day?
- What beliefs or fears keep me from fully receiving love?
- In what ways can I open my heart more toward others?
- How can I embody Divine love in my daily interactions?
- What would my life feel like if I truly believed, "I am love"?

Affirmation

"I am created from Divine love."
"I am worthy of love, and I give and receive it freely."
"I release fear and allow love to flow through me."
"Love surrounds me, fills me, and expresses itself through me in all that I do."

Boundaries

We build boundaries to create protection, space, and privacy for ourselves. A boundary is a clear understanding of what feels acceptable and respectful to you, and what does not. It is not a wall meant to shut others out, but a guideline that defines how you allow yourself to be treated and how you choose to show up in return.

At the same time, if boundaries become too rigid, they can prevent meaningful connection. The key is balance, a healthy structure that honors your private thoughts, space, and well-being, while still leaving room for genuine interaction and closeness with others.

Boundaries are deeply personal. What is important to you might not matter to someone else, and vice versa. Do not assume where someone else's boundaries lie, for you cannot know what they have experienced throughout their life. Some people are born outspoken and clear, while others prefer being quiet and private. Both ways are equally valid; one is not better than the other. Boundaries grow out of lived experiences, lessons, and belief systems, and it is important to be aware of them — not only for yourself but also for those who encounter you.

We build boundaries to create protection, space, and privacy for ourselves. At the same time, if boundaries are too rigid, they can keep us from forming meaningful connections. The key is balance — a healthy structure that honors your private thoughts, space, and energy, while leaving room for genuine interaction and closeness with others.

When you take the time to define your boundaries, you gain clarity about what you are willing to compromise on and what you are not. Boundaries may show up differently depending on the relationship. The boundaries you hold with a partner, a family member, a friend, or a colleague are not the same, yet they are guided by the same inner values.

Examples of boundaries include choosing how much time and energy you give to others, deciding what topics feel safe to discuss, and recognizing when you need space rather than engagement. They may involve saying no without guilt, limiting contact that feels draining, or expressing your needs clearly instead of remaining silent to keep the peace. Honor yourself enough to respect your limits and protect your truth. Stand firmly by what matters most to you. In doing so, you not only care for yourself, but you also teach others how to treat you.

When you live authentically within your boundaries, others either align with your energy or drift away. This is not a matter of blame or judgment, but simply a natural separation of energies that do not match. As your boundaries begin to mirror your inner truth, a quiet freedom emerges, the freedom to live and relate as your authentic self. What a great gift this is, both to you and to the world. When you shine brightly, others want to be near you and follow suit. This can have a powerful impact on the world, so go for it, establish guidelines that will help you shine.

Reflection
- Where in your life have you allowed others to cross your boundaries?
- Which boundaries feel firm and healthy for you, and which feel too rigid or too loose?
- How does honoring your boundaries change the way you feel about yourself and your relationships?

Affirmation
*"I honor my truth by setting clear and loving boundaries.
I am free to be myself."*

Faith

Faith, by definition, is not something we can see, feel, or touch. We either have it, or you don't. Having faith means believing in something greater than ourselves. It allows us to hold hope when life feels heavy, and it gives us the strength to get up and keep going, trusting that a higher power will assist you along the way. Faith reminds us that we are not alone, that there is a force, a strength, and a support system guiding us toward where we are meant to be.

Do not limit yourself to believing there is only one supreme source. Whoever you feel most connected to—whether it is God, Jesus, Buddha, Mohammed, Yahweh, or Abraham, remember that we are also surrounded by personal guides, angels, archangels, spirits, crossed-over loved ones, and even beings from other dimensions. At any moment, you can call upon them.

It takes practice to connect with these guides, and yes, it takes faith. How can you call on something unseen without believing there will be an answer? You may not hear or see them right away, but you might sense a shift, an insight, a sudden thought, an urge to act, or a feeling of warmth and reassurance. You might hear a song, notice a sign, or feel a gentle tingle. These are all ways the other side reaches out to you. With patience and trust, communication becomes clearer over time.

Every one of us has the ability to connect with the unseen world. You are part of it, just as it is part of you. You might think, "*No, I can't* "or *"That's not for me,"* but yes, you can. It is simply a matter of quieting the mind, opening your intuition, and allowing faith to guide you.

Faith is a two-way street. To experience peace and trust, you must be willing to release control. Faith asks you to believe in something bigger than yourself, something you can't measure or hold. It is that spark of hope that lights your way when everything feels dark. But faith is a two-way street. To experience peace and trust, you must be willing to release control. Without faith, life can feel lonely or stagnant, as if you're walking in circles. However, when times are difficult and you don't know where to turn, faith reminds you that you are never truly lost.

Having faith doesn't make you blind or naïve. It's much like love. You can't see or touch love, yet you trust that it exists. You sense it through words, actions, and energy. To truly receive it, you must have faith in both yourself and the other person. Faith works the same way—you trust in something larger than life itself, something unseen yet ever-present. It surrounds you with acceptance, love, and belonging.

Faith gives you the courage to keep moving forward, even when the path is unclear. Be bold, have faith, and step into the unknown. The light will meet you there.

Reflection

- Think of a time when you felt completely lost or uncertain, yet something unseen helped you find your way.
- What role did faith play in that moment?
- How can you lean into that same trust now, when challenges arise?

Affirmation

"I trust the unseen forces of love and guidance that surround me. My faith lights the path before me, even in times of uncertainty."

Trust

At some point in life, all of us are asked to face the question of trust. We may struggle to trust ourselves, find it difficult to trust others because we feel unworthy, or carry wounds from betrayal that make trusting again feel risky or even impossible.

At its core, trust is tied to our most basic human needs, the need to belong, to feel accepted, nurtured, and safe, to have a soft place to land. When these needs are met, trust has room to grow. Slowly, gently, we begin to open again and allow others closer.

If you were fortunate enough to grow up in a nurturing, supportive, and loving environment, trust may have developed naturally for you. But when those elements were missing, trust does not form easily. In those cases, rebuilding trust becomes conscious work, both with yourself and with others. Trust can only exist where there is safety, acceptance, and reciprocity. It is never one-sided. It must flow both ways and be honored over time.

Life has a way of revealing where trust lives and where it does not. Many of us have experienced moments where we believed someone was trustworthy, only to feel deeply disappointed or betrayed. These moments can be devastating. When trust is broken, the pain often cuts far deeper than we expect. The real question becomes, how do we respond?

Betrayal, especially within close or intimate relationships, can leave us feeling hollow, defeated, and wounded. And yet, even here, we are not powerless. We always have a choice. We can cling to the story, replay the hurt, and allow the betrayal to define us. Or we can acknowledge what happened, learn from it, release what no longer serves us, and choose a different way forward.

Many people become trapped in mental replay, reliving the moment again and again. This loop keeps the wound alive and often leads to isolation, depression, and a deepening sense of distrust. But when you choose, and yes, it is a choice, to release the emotional weight, something shifts. Strength returns. Resilience grows. Space opens for healing and new experiences.

When trust is broken early in life, especially in childhood, the impact is profound. A child's sense of safety, love, and predictability disappears, leaving confusion about whether people exist to protect or to harm. Children who experience abuse, abandonment, or emotional neglect often internalize the pain. They ask themselves, *"What did I do wrong? "or "What is wrong with me?"* Shame and self-doubt take root. But the truth matters here, deeply. The betrayal was never the child's fault. The responsibility belongs solely to the one who crossed the line. Your inner child is innocent.

Healing begins when you stop carrying a burden that was never yours to carry and gently begin to open your heart again.

Choosing to trust, to create your own sense of safety, and to move forward is how you reclaim your life. To do otherwise is to remain stuck in cycles of pain, confusion, anger, and denial. When you stay there, the person who hurt you still holds power over your life. But when you forgive, not forget, and release the grip the past has on you, you step into your own authority. You are no longer defined by what happened. You free yourself to grow, to love, and to trust again.

I know this path intimately. I was abused at a very young age by an extended family member. That experience left a deep imprint, and for many years, I struggled with self-acceptance and trust. Today, at fifty-seven, I can honestly say I am doing well. I have come a long way. Trust will likely always be a tender subject for me, but I live with an open heart. I trust myself, and I trust others. I know now that I am strong enough to face whatever life brings.

The turning point came when I decided that the past would no longer define my life. Making that decision was simple. Living it was not. There were moments when I wanted to give up, when the work felt overwhelming. But I stayed. I persevered.

It took me seven years to work through my pain, rebuild my sense of safety, and learn to trust again, especially men. To understand the depth of that journey, know this, at twenty-one, I married my husband and moved from Europe to the United States. That alone required immense trust. I loved him deeply, yet I struggled, not because he gave me reason to doubt him, but because I did not yet trust myself. I feared that if he truly saw all of me, he would not love or accept me. At the time, I did not believe I was worthy.

Now, after almost thirty-six years of marriage, I can say with confidence that we have worked through our differences. I trust him fully. And just as importantly, I trust myself, to love and to receive love. Our relationship has grown stronger over time. It has depth, resilience, and truth.

I invite you to open your heart and trust that you are capable of loving and protecting yourself. When you believe in your own strength, you move through the world differently, grounded, resilient, and open, even in the presence of pain or uncertainty. Trust begins within. And when it is rooted there, it allows you to build meaningful, connected relationships, with yourself first, and then with others.

Reflection

- Where in your life do you struggle most with trust, yourself, others, or life itself?
- Which past experiences still influence how you trust today?
- How does your body feel when your heart is open versus when it is guarded?

- What small step can you take today to rebuild trust from within?

Affirmation

"I trust the wisdom of my heart."
"I release fear and open myself to love, safety, and truth."
"I am worthy of trust, within myself and with others."

Allowing

Everything unfolds in divine timing. When you allow life to move in its natural rhythm, things begin to soften. Life feels less heavy, less forced. This does not mean it becomes effortless, but it does become clearer. Allowing asks you to release the need to push, manage, or control every outcome.

In the physical world, this is not always easy. The ego-mind is quick to remind us that we must stay in control, that we cannot rely on others, and that everything depends on us alone. Yet when we slow down and step back, we often discover that many things resolve themselves without our constant interference. They may not unfold the way we imagined or hoped, but they do unfold. And often, they do so in ways that serve us better than we could have planned.

Your presence here is not accidental. You are surrounded by people, places, and experiences that appear in their own perfect timing. There are no mistakes. Every encounter, every detour, every pause carries meaning. While you have free will, the Universe continues to support and guide you toward your highest good. You are exactly where you are meant to be right now. If you were meant to be somewhere else, you would be. It truly is that simple.

Still, many of us believe we must solve everything ourselves. We struggle to trust that life will work out without constant effort or control. Yet every experience carries a lesson, an invitation for your soul to grow and expand. When you step back and allow, the

Universe responds by placing the right people and situations in your path, often without them even realizing the role they are playing in your growth.

Allowing is a gift you give yourself. It means accepting where you are, living fully in the present moment, and trusting that what unfolds next will serve your highest good. This is not passivity. Allowing is an active form of trust. It takes strength to release control and surrender to the flow, especially when the outcome is unclear. But the unfolding is already in motion. You are supported more than you realize.

Wayne Dyer captured this beautifully when he said that the word *ego* stands for Edge God Out. He once shared the example of a baby growing in the womb. For nine months, everything unfolds perfectly. Cells divide, organs form, life takes shape. We do not interfere. We trust the process completely. Yet once the baby is born, we suddenly feel the need to control everything.

Isn't this also how we approach our own lives?

Do you trust that life is unfolding in your favor? Can you believe that even when you cannot see the outcome, things are still working out as they should? Are you willing to loosen your grip, just a little, and allow life to reveal itself without needing all the answers?

You do not need to fix everything. You do not need to carry the weight of the world on your shoulders. You do not need to know how it will all come together. In time, it always does. When you allow yourself to be guided by a higher intelligence, you arrive exactly where you are meant to be, at the moment you are meant to be there.

And in that allowing, you find peace.

Reflection

- Where in your life are you trying to control the outcome instead of allowing it to unfold?
- How does your body feel when you force compared to when you allow?

- What might shift if you trusted that everything is unfolding in divine order, even without visible proof?
- What part of your life is asking you to surrender and soften right now?

Affirmation
"I allow life to unfold in perfect timing."
"I trust that I am guided, supported, and exactly where I am meant to be."

Wisdom

Wisdom lives within you. It is cultivated through knowledge, experience, and time. While some seem naturally attuned to it, wisdom cannot be rushed or forced. It unfolds gradually, shaped by life itself. You grow into it through reflection, patience, and a willingness to learn and living through life events. Many begin the journey, but not everyone fully arrives.

Masters and sages are often recognized for their wisdom because they have learned, over many years, how to respond rather than react. They observe before they speak. They pause before they act. And sometimes, they choose silence. There is immense power in silence. It allows clarity to rise and truth to settle before words are formed.

Through experience and discipline, these individuals learn self-mastery. They move through life with a sense of inner steadiness, remaining unattached to outcomes while still fully present. Rather than reacting to the world around them, they observe from within. Their understanding comes from the inside out, not from external circumstances.

Younger souls, or those earlier on their path, often become entangled in the drama of life. They may believe that involvement gives them meaning, identity, or validation. They are quick to speak, quick to react, quick to defend their opinions. This is not wrong; it is simply part of learning. But wisdom reveals itself through listening, watching, and discerning when to speak, and when not to. A master walks in knowing. A student continues to seek outside themselves. The difference is subtle but profound. One trusts inner truth; the other is still searching for it externally.

So how do you know whether something is truly right for you, or merely an opinion you have absorbed from others? The answer is always within. Take time to listen to your inner voice, your unique rhythm, your own quiet knowing. Learn from others, yes. Read, explore, ask questions. But do not lose yourself in the noise of external validation. You already hold the wisdom you seek.

To walk in your own wisdom is a form of freedom. When you trust yourself, you move through life with calm confidence and inner strength. You stop outsourcing your truth and begin relying on your own inner resources. This shift opens a new way of being, one grounded in peace, clarity, and self-empowerment. And once this trust is established, it becomes part of who you are. It cannot be taken from you unless you choose to give it away.

Trust your intuition, it often speaks in quiet nudges and subtle inner knowing. Yet intuition is only the beginning. Wisdom grows deeper, shaped by lived experience, reflection, and discernment.

When you honor your gifts and listen inwardly, you begin to integrate both. Intuition guides you in the moment, while wisdom helps you understand what that guidance means. Together, they form a steady foundation beneath your choices.

As you walk in your own wisdom, you gradually return to yourself. And in that return, you discover a freedom that does not depend on circumstances, but on alignment with who you truly are.

Reflection

Think of a time when you sought guidance from others, only to later realize the answer was already within you.

What helped you recognize your own wisdom?

How did trusting yourself change the outcome?

Affirmation

"I trust my inner voice and honor my own wisdom."
"All that I need to know already lives within me."

Life's Challenges

The moments that feel most challenging in your life are often the ones most essential to your growth. These experiences are not random. They appear on your path for a reason, inviting you to endure, to learn, and ultimately to rise. The Universe, or Source, uses these moments to help you remember who you are and to bring clarity to your purpose in this lifetime.

Each time you move through frustration, anger, sadness, or disillusionment and come out the other side, something within you shifts. Your vibration rises. This shift does not affect only you; it quietly influences those around you as well. Your resilience becomes a silent teacher, showing others what is possible. As they witness your growth, their own awareness may begin to expand.

When you begin to notice and reflect on these sensations, you strengthen your trust in your inner guidance. Every person you encounter carries their own vibration. Sometimes it harmonizes naturally with yours, and at other times it clashes, creating discomfort. This has little to do with personality or words. Someone may say all the right things, yet your body responds with tension or unease. In those moments, awareness matters. You are invited to decide whether to keep this person within your energetic space or to step back in order to protect your well-being.

Life's challenges often emerge not through dramatic events, but through the steady accumulation of pressure. A demanding job, ongoing conflict, or prolonged uncertainty can gradually wear you down. Tasks that once felt manageable begin to feel heavy. Your patience shortens. Your body holds tension that does not fully release. Over time, these experiences deplete your emotional and physical reserves, leaving you fatigued, disconnected, and less present in your own life.

Other challenges unfold within relationships. Navigating boundaries, feeling misunderstood, or carrying responsibilities that are not truly yours can slowly erode your inner steadiness. You may overextend yourself, silence your needs, or push beyond your limits in an effort to maintain harmony. While these patterns may feel necessary in the moment, they gradually diminish your clarity, vitality, and sense of self.

Recognizing how life's challenges affect you is not weakness, it is awareness. When you begin to notice what drains you and what restores you, you reclaim the ability to respond with intention rather than react from exhaustion.

Discernment becomes especially important during challenging moments, when your choices matter most. You are not powerless in these situations. You are the captain of your life, and you have the right to decide who and what you allow into your inner world. Trusting these internal cues helps you navigate life with greater awareness, protecting your well-being while staying true to yourself.

Ask yourself: *"What kind of world do I want to live in?"* One shaped by anger, negativity, and despair, or one rooted in kindness, joy, and beauty? The choice is always yours. You are the one who assigns meaning to what you see, hear, and experience.

By taking time to reflect on your emotions, thoughts, and actions, you gain the ability to shift your energy at any moment. The power to change direction is always within your reach. When you choose to raise your vibration, you not only support your own healing, but you also contribute to the healing of the collective. For you to thrive, self-reflection must become a daily practice. Go inward and discover your truth and trust that when challenges come your way your inner guidance will lead you to success.

Reflection

Think of a recent challenge that tested your strength or patience. What lesson might it have carried for your growth?

How did you respond, and how might you respond differently next time to raise your vibration?

Affirmation

"Every challenge I face strengthens me and deepens my awareness."
"I rise with grace, and my light quietly uplifts the world around me."

Silence

Meeting yourself in silence is one of life's most profound experiences. For many, however, it can also feel unsettling. Without distraction, stillness brings forward thoughts and emotions we might prefer to avoid. Yet it is precisely within that discomfort that peace begins to reveal itself.

In today's world, constant stimulation has become the norm. Television, music, phones, and endless to-do lists keep us perpetually occupied. While this busyness may feel productive or comforting, it often pulls us further away from ourselves. We stay connected to everything except our own inner world.

Silence requires courage. It removes the protection that noise provides. It is a doorway to the soul and a tool of immeasurable power. Its effects reach far beyond the quiet moment itself. This is why meditation can be so transformative. In stillness, you attune not only to your own essence, but also to the greater rhythm of the Universe. Silence is where connection lives, where guidance is received, and where clarity gently rises without force.

When you learn to meet silence without fear, it becomes a trusted ally. It is always available, always waiting. Accessing it takes patience and practice, but once you cross that threshold, you can return to it whenever needed. In silence, wisdom does not need to be chased, it arises naturally. It becomes your compass, your rudder, your quiet sense of direction. When you embrace silence, you are never truly lost. Life is challenging enough; you do not need to navigate it without support.

Create space for stillness in whatever way feels natural to you, through meditation, long walks, journaling, or quiet moments alone in nature. The Spirit Realm is always ready to assist, but to hear its guidance, your vibration must be receptive. Silence is the pathway that allows this alignment to occur.

The difference between prayer and meditation is simple. In prayer, you speak. In silence, you listen.

In stillness, you hear the wisdom of the Universe. In trust, you follow where it leads.

You are the one who decides, noise or peace, distraction or clarity. One keeps you circling in the same patterns; the other gently sets you free. When you truly spend time in silence and listen, you will recognize what your soul has been choosing all along.

Reflection

- Take a few moments to sit in complete stillness. Turn off distractions. Close your eyes. Breathe.
- Notice what arises when the noise fades. Do certain thoughts, memories, or emotions surface?
- Instead of pushing them away, observe them gently, without judgment. Ask yourself:
- What does silence reveal to me today?
- Where in my life could I invite more stillness?
- When was the last time I truly listened, to myself, to others, or to the quiet guidance within?

Write down whatever comes forward. Sometimes the message is subtle; other times it is profound. Either way, it is your soul speaking. Listen with kindness.

Affirmation

"In silence, I meet myself."
"In stillness, I hear the voice of my soul."
"I trust the guidance that rises within me, for it speaks in the language of the Divine."
"Peace lives within me, and I return to it with ease and gratitude."

Family

Family is our first connection to the world, the foundation from which our life's journey begins. This early bond can be one of warmth and security, or it can be marked by volatility and uncertainty. Either way, it leaves an imprint.

When family relationships are loving and stable, they provide a safe space to explore life and grow. Even as infants, we sense this security on a deep, unconscious level. Babies are deeply attuned to their environment, they feel tension and disharmony immediately and respond accordingly, long before they can understand it with words. Safety, or the lack of it, is absorbed before language ever forms.

When the family environment is unstable, fear and withdrawal often take root. These early experiences can leave lasting impressions, shaping how we view ourselves and the world around us. Over time, they influence our relationships, our choices, and even our physical, emotional, and spiritual well-being. The good news is that once we become aware of these patterns, we are no longer powerless. Awareness opens the door to healing and transformation.

When I look back at my own life, I can see how early family dynamics shaped the way I moved through the world. Growing up in an environment where stability was not always guaranteed, I learned to stay alert, to anticipate shifts in mood, and to adapt quickly. At the time, these responses felt necessary. They helped me navigate uncertainty and maintain a sense of control.

But as I grew older, I began to notice how those same patterns followed me into adulthood. I overextended myself in relationships, took responsibility for emotions that were not mine, and struggled to fully relax, even in safe environments. What once served as protection had quietly become limitation.

It was only when I became aware of these patterns that something began to shift. I realized I could honor where they came from without allowing them to define how I continued forward. Awareness gave me the opportunity to respond differently, to create new patterns rooted not in fear, but in intention.

Healing is a deeply personal process, and its timing is different for each of us. There is no deadline, no single path that fits everyone. Yet, if we wish to change the trajectory of our lives, we must be willing to engage with it. This means acknowledging the past with honesty, releasing the past, and consciously choosing new ways of thinking and being as we move forward.

We cannot choose our family, but we can choose how we relate to them. It is both healthy and necessary to set boundaries when needed, even if social or cultural conditioning tells you otherwise. Remember, you are your own spark of energy, a sovereign being in your own right. Your life is yours to shape, not according to what others expect of you or family obligations, but according to who you choose to become.

Letting go of the need to live according to your family's expectations can be challenging, especially when loyalty and love are intertwined. Loving your family does not require self-abandonment. You can honor who they are and where they are on their own journey while still giving yourself permission to walk your own path. This is not an act of rejection, but one of self-respect.

Living authentically, with freedom and integrity, is the greatest gift you can give yourself. And when you choose to live in alignment with your truth, you often give others permission to do the same. Healing within the family does not always mean staying close, but it always means staying true to yourself.

Reflection

Take a moment to reflect on your family story and how it has shaped the person you are today.

- Which family patterns or beliefs have supported your growth?
- Which ones have held you back?

Then ask yourself:

- What role did I play in my family dynamic growing up?
- What have I learned from those experiences?
- What do I need to forgive or release to create peace within myself?
- What kind of "family energy" do I want to cultivate moving forward, with relatives, friends, and my chosen family?

Write freely and without judgment. Healing begins with awareness and the willingness to view your story with compassion.

Affirmation

"I honor where I come from, but I am not bound by my past."
"I release the patterns that no longer serve me and create space for peace and love."
"I choose to relate to family members with compassion, authenticity, and freedom."
"My family story shaped me, but my spirit defines me."

Unresolved Anger

Unresolved anger often stems from painful emotions experienced in the past. At some point, everyone is confronted with unresolved feelings, and for many, they surface as anger. Yet anger is often the easiest, and most superficial, way of dealing with deeper emotions. When we react in anger, it is wise to pause and redirect our attention toward the true source of pain, focusing on understanding and resolution rather than justification, or worse, displacing it onto those closest to us.

When anger surfaces, pause and ask yourself, "*What am I really angry about?*" Most of the time, the person or situation in front of you is not the true source. They are merely the catalyst, a mirror inviting you to face emotions that have not yet been fully processed. The solution does not exist outside of you. It lives within.

Healing takes time, honesty, and courage. Often, we unknowingly stand in our own way and, at times, even sabotage our progress. Expectations, especially the ones we place upon ourselves, are another common source of anger. When it arises, ask yourself, "*Were my expectations realistic? Was I unconsciously trying to fill a need within myself through another person or situation?*"

Many people are unaware of the true roots of their anger. We lash out without pausing to understand why. But the truth is, no one else *makes* us angry. We choose how we respond, whether consciously or unconsciously, and we are ultimately responsible for our reactions.

Unresolved anger does not remain confined to the mind. It settles into the body. I witness this often in Reiki sessions, clients come in with back pain, stomach issues, or shoulder tension that, from an energetic perspective, is frequently linked to unhealed emotions. Over time, stored anger can manifest as physical discomfort or dis-ease.

True healing requires the willingness to go inward and ask the difficult questions. When you release what you have been holding onto, both your body and soul become lighter. Letting go of anger and stored tension brings a sense of freedom, flexibility, and renewed vitality. Love yourself enough to do this inner work. As you do, peace follows naturally, and as your energy rises, similar energy begins to flow into your life.

Anger creates suffering. Yet behind anger lies the key to your freedom. When you are willing to move beneath it, to uncover the truth it is guarding, you reclaim your power. Anger tends to multiply itself, while calmness invites peace and clarity. Within this peace, you are free to be yourself and to shape a life that feels aligned, authentic, and whole.

Reflection

- What unresolved emotions might be hiding beneath your anger?
- Are there recurring people or situations that trigger the same reaction? What might they be reflecting back to you?
- Where in your body do you feel tension or discomfort when anger arises?
- What might change if you responded with awareness rather than reacting automatically?

Affirmation

"I release anger and the need to control outcomes."
"I am willing to see the truth beneath my emotions and let go with love."
"Peace flows through me, calming my mind and soothing my body."
"I am free, centered, and at peace within myself."

The Sun

The Sun equals life. It gives energy to everything that exists. Without the Sun, nothing on Earth could grow, bloom, or continue to live. From the smallest cell to the largest tree, from animals to human beings, all of life responds to the light of the Sun.

Since the earliest times, people have honored the Sun. The Egyptians worshipped Ra, the Sun God, as the giver of life. The Incas revered Inti, their Sun deity, with equal devotion. Even today, we feel the Sun's power deeply. After a long winter, when the Sun finally breaks through the clouds, we feel renewed. The colors of the world look brighter, the air feels fresher, and our energy returns.

Science confirms what we intuitively know: without sunlight and vitamin D, our health suffers. Low energy, sadness, or even depression can arise from a lack of exposure to the Sun. Yet with its light, we feel recharged, alive, and inspired to begin again.

The Sun reminds us of the eternal cycle of duality, endings and beginnings, darkness and light, rest and renewal. The Sun rises every morning, chasing away the night, giving us hope for a new day. Indigenous peoples across the world have long honored this sacred rhythm, understanding that the Sun is both a physical and spiritual source of nourishment.

Take a moment each day to honor the Sun. Offer gratitude for its warmth, its life-giving rays, and its role in the cycle of renewal. Without change, life would become dull and stagnant. But with the Sun's guidance, we are shown the beauty in constant transformation.

Remember, it is worth noting that the energy of the Sun also lives within each of us. It fills every cell of our bodies with life. When you feel depleted, step outside, breathe in the light, and allow it to refuel you. Notice its energy in the plants, the flowers, and the world around us. The more you practice connecting with this energy, the more you can use it to uplift yourself whenever we need it.

Honor the Sun, honor the Earth, and honor yourself, for you, too, carry that same light.

Reflection

- When was the last time you paused to truly feel the warmth of the Sun on your skin?
- What emotions arise when you think of the Sun's energy—renewal, joy, gratitude, peace?
- How can you bring more light into your daily life, both literally and metaphorically?
- In what ways can you honor the light within yourself just as you honor the light of the Sun?

Take a few moments to sit quietly in sunlight, even if only by a window. Breathe deeply, allowing that light to enter and energize every part of you.

Affirmation

"The light of the Sun shines within me."
"I honor the warmth, renewal, and energy it brings to my life."
"I am radiant, balanced, and filled with Divine light."
"The same energy that lights the world also lights my soul."

Happiness

Happiness is a state of mind, created by our own choice. Happiness is not something outside of you; it is something we allow yourselves to experience. Every day, you can choose to move toward happiness or move away from it.

Many people become caught up in drama, whether from others or from their own thoughts. When we give away our energy to drama, happiness eludes us. We cannot exist in drama and happiness at the same time. Only a calm and balanced mind can experience true joy.

Happiness does not mean life will be perfect. Challenges will still appear, but you have the power to choose how you respond. You are not your body alone; you are a spiritual being having a physical experience. From that higher perspective, you can tap into your inner strength and create joy even in the midst of change.

At any given moment, you can redirect your energy. Take a deep breath, center yourself, and step back from the situation. You can see yourself as an eagle flying high, watching from above, and ask yourself: *"What outcome do I want to create here?"* From that space, you can respond in a way that supports peace and happiness, instead of being pulled into negativity.

The truth running through this book is simple yet powerful: you are the creator of your own life. You have the power to shape your thoughts, your actions, and your experiences. And most important of all, you can switch your thoughts from negative to positive in the blink of an eye. That is your strength. That is your power.

Happiness is not something you stumble upon; it is something you cultivate and choose again and again. When you live from this choice, you bring peace to your mind, harmony to your surroundings, and lightness to your heart. Happiness is your birthright. Claim it.

Reflection

- When was the last time you felt truly happy, and what contributed to that feeling?
- Are there areas in your life where drama or negativity still pull your attention?
- How might you shift your energy when faced with frustration or stress?
- What daily practices help you return to a state of inner joy?

Affirmation

"Happiness lives within me. I choose to nurture peace, gratitude, and joy in every moment of my life."

Synchronicity

Synchronicity happens when events align in unexpected ways, without any prior planning, and often when you least expect it. These moments may catch us off guard, yet they carry a deeper meaning. They are reminders that the Universe is always working with us, not against us.

As I write these words, I am reminded of a moment that illustrates this clearly. One morning, I felt the urge to meditate and joined an online session led by Master Stephen Co, the current leader of Pranic® Healing. The meditation left me feeling centered and open. Less than ten minutes after it ended, I received a phone call from a friend I had met two years earlier. Although we had stayed in occasional contact, we had not seen each other in person for quite some time. She called to ask if I would be interested in starting a mediumship circle and development workshop together.

What made this moment significant was not just the timing, but the way the invitation mirrored the inner state I had just entered through meditation, focused, receptive, and aligned with my deeper interests. We agreed to meet bi-weekly, and with the benefit of hindsight, that circle continued for almost five years.

The synchronicity in this moment was clear: by raising my vibration through meditation, I opened myself to new energy and experiences. In meditation, you forgive, let go, and release, creating space for what is meant to arrive. The Universe responded immediately. These moments reminded me that I am not alone and that life itself is in cooperation with not just me, but each of us.

Synchronicity is a sign that you are on the right track. It is the Universe's way of saying, *"Well done, here is your reward, use it to grow and keep moving forward."* Our human perspective is limited, but the Universe sees the greater picture and nudges us beyond our comfort zone, guiding us toward becoming a greater version of ourselves.

Trust the synchronicities that show up on your path. They are not random coincidences; they are opportunities for growth. While free will allows you to ignore them, choosing to embrace these moments creates a richer, more meaningful life. By raising your vibration and setting the tone for synchronicities to unfold, you align yourself with joy, guidance, and purpose. As you move into the light, synchronicity becomes your guide, leading you toward what your soul is ready to experience. Trust the process and allow your life to unfold in divine order. The Universe has plans you cannot even imagine for yourself, so when you are pushed out of your comfort zone, jump.

Reflection

Think back to a time when something "just fell into place" unexpectedly, a call, a meeting, a turn of events that felt divinely timed. What were you feeling, thinking, or doing just before it happened? Write about that moment and how it may have guided or supported your growth. Then ask yourself: *"What can I do to stay open to synchronicity in my daily life?"*

Affirmation

*"I trust the flow of life and recognize the signs that guide me.
I am aligned with divine timing, and everything unfolds
for my highest good."*

Expectations

Expectations are born from the desire to control. We seek control over our lives, our environment, and even the lives of others. Expectations are not based on reality, yet they hold great power over us. An expectation is an idea or emotion about what we believe we should receive from ourselves or others.

When these expectations are not met, disappointment often follows. At times, this can spiral into disillusionment or even depression. Our expectations are shaped by our conditioning, by our family, culture, or community, all of which influence how we view the world and how we "box in" others and ourselves. When we project these expectations onto others, we attempt to control their behavior or the outcome of a situation. Nine times out of ten, our expectations are not fulfilled, leaving us feeling discouraged and wanting.

To free yourself from expectations is to recognize that they are not tangible realities. Expectations have no form. They exist as mental constructs, shaped by imagination and conditioned patterns of thought that keep us circling the same experiences. When we place these internal expectations on ourselves or others, we limit growth and create unnecessary strain.

This is different from practical agreements or shared responsibilities, such as mutual expectations around behavior, commitments, or obligations within families, relationships, workplaces, or society. Releasing imagined outcomes does not mean abandoning responsibility. It means allowing life to unfold without forcing it into a predetermined shape. In doing so, you create space for trust, growth, and what is truly meant to emerge.

Each person has their own individual lessons to learn, independent of anyone else. When you burden others with your expectations, you interfere with their growth and expansion. You have control only over your own life, your thoughts, your actions, and your choices. It is not your role to judge or reject another person for the path they walk, because you cannot know the experiences that shaped them into who they are today.

Release expectations by living in the present moment. Expectations are projections into the future, mental images of how you believe something should unfold. When you bring your attention back to what is happening right now, those imagined outcomes lose their grip, and you respond to reality as it is rather than to a story in your mind.

Accept what is in this moment and trust the unfolding process. We are all on this dance floor of life, each moving to a different rhythm, yet sharing the same space. When you allow life to unfold without rushing in with judgment or fixed opinions, you create room for authentic growth, both your own and that of others.

Imagine the change that could take place if every person lived authentically, not trying to meet false expectations but simply being who they are meant to be. The world would be filled with truth, light, and positivity instead of the constant bombardment of drama, negativity, and falsehoods.

Let your focus rest on yourself. Become the person you wish to become and release the need to expect anything from others. Embody the energy of the life you want to live, even before it fully manifests. Expect only the best of yourself, and embrace both your strengths and your weaknesses, for they shape who you are. Do not compare yourself to others; your uniqueness is your power and your gift. When you walk in your full, authentic energy, life opens to you.

Synchronicity flows, wonder returns, and your path becomes one of joy and fulfillment.

Reflection

- What expectations am I holding onto myself or of others that create frustration or disappointment?
- How might life feel if I released these expectations and trusted the unfolding of events?
- Am I living authentically, or am I trying to live up to someone else's idea of me?

Affirmation

"I release expectations and allow life to unfold in perfect alignment, with trust, openness, and authenticity."

Opposites

Light and dark, opposites we are all familiar with. Yet we need both in order to comprehend each concept individually. Without dark, we would not see light, and without light, we cannot understand the dark. Each exists on its own, but without the other, we would have no reference point, no way to differentiate.

Our planet is one of duality, meaning that for every action, there is an equal and opposite reaction.

- Where there is darkness, light makes it recede.
- Where things are wet, they cannot be dry.
- Where there is heat, there is no cold.

To experience each concept fully, we must understand both sides of the equation. Like a pendulum, we swing back and forth, minute to minute, hour to hour, from day to day. Sometimes we swing too far in one direction, and at other times too far in the other. The key is to return to the middle path. Walking in balance allows us to live in harmony, like a wagon wheel rolling steadily along a road. Sometimes you rise, sometimes you descend, yet the movement continues forward. Progress is not found in staying at the top or avoiding the bottom, but in allowing both to exist as part of the journey.

Life unfolds through opposites, light and dark, strength and vulnerability, certainty and doubt. Each gives meaning to the other. Without contrast, growth would not be possible. When you learn to accept both sides rather than resist one in favor of the other, you remain centered even as circumstances shift. Balance is not the absence of change; it is the willingness to move with it. And in that movement, you continue forward toward your destination.

Walking in balance allows us to live in harmony, like a wagon wheel rolling steadily along a road. Sometimes you are up, sometimes you go down, but you are always moving forward toward your destination.

When you stop resisting the energetic flow of duality and begin to understand the ebb and flow of life, serenity becomes yours. Allow life to unfold. Accept what comes your way and keep moving forward. The Universe has a plan far greater than anything you could imagine, so trust the process. Trust the process, knowing that life moves through opposites, expansion and contraction, light and shadow, each guiding you forward in ways you may not yet understand.

We are all energetically connected. What you send out, you receive in return. Light attracts light, darkness attracts darkness, negativity attracts negativity, and positivity attracts positivity. This is the law of vibration and resonance in the Universe.

There is a light within you that shines constantly. This light radiates a vibrational frequency out into the Universe, which in turn reflects it back to you. If you feel low or drained, go within and connect to your light, it is always there to guide you in the right direction. You can choose to shine this light outward or keep it to yourself. When you choose to share it, your presence alone uplifts others, whether they are aware of it or not. They might not recognize it consciously, but they will certainly feel the energy.

By shifting your frequency, through your thoughts, actions, and energy, you choose how brightly your light shines. The brighter your inner light, the more goodness you attract. People are naturally drawn to light, just as moths are drawn to a flame. When you choose to live consciously and radiate your inner light, you not only uplift yourself but also positively affect everyone around you.

As you consider the balance of opposites in your own life, take a moment to reflect on how you walk your path.

Reflection
- Where in your life do you notice yourself swinging to extremes rather than walking the middle path?
- How do you respond when life feels "up" versus when it feels "down"?
- What would balance look like for you in daily living?

Affirmation

"I embrace the dance of light and dark, knowing both serve my growth. I walk the middle path with grace, trust, and balance."

Sound

Sound is vibration, and vibration carries information. Even your own voice carries an energetic frequency unique to you. The energy in our bodies, when combined with the sound of your voice, it becomes your personal vibration, your unique sound.

Your vibration shapes your path and can bring healing or contribute to illness. We have all felt discomfort in the presence of negative vibrations such as certain people, places, or events. They can feel heavy or unsettling, and we want to run the other way. Likewise, we have all felt uplifted in environments filled with music, laughter, or peace, inviting us in and making us feel welcome. The difference between these experiences lies in vibration.

Sound can reshape cells, alter energy, and shift your vibrational state. It can change your mood from negative to positive in an instant. Since we are beings of vibration, sound influences our physical, emotional, and spiritual well-being. Sound waves naturally form sacred geometric patterns, bringing harmony and healing to the body. Today, sound therapy is even used in hospitals during surgery to support the body's natural healing process.

We have all experienced moments when music transported us beyond the physical world. We know the feeling when a song, a tone, or even the sound of a baby crying or a cat purring stirs something deep within. Sound connects with us far beyond the surface.

The Japanese researcher Masaru Emoto demonstrated the influence of sound on water molecules beautifully. He exposed water samples to different words and sounds, then froze the water and photographed the crystals. The results were amazing: positive words created beautifully formed, harmonious structures, whereas negative words produced distorted, fragmented shapes. Since humans are made up of more than seventy percent water, imagine how sound and words affect us on every level. Yes! Even when planets emit their own sounds, NASA has recorded the vibrations of the moon and other celestial bodies, reminding us that the Universe itself is alive with music and motion.

If you are feeling low, turn to sound. Play a song that uplifts you. Step into nature and listen to the birds, the wind moving through the trees, and even the stillness between sounds. These vibrations soothe the soul and bring relaxation and renewal.

Incorporate sound into your daily life. Allow your body to heal and let sound energize and uplift you. Sound is not just heard, it is felt deep within, and it has the power to transform your being.

Take time each day to include sound in your routine to renew your soul. Whether through music, words, or the natural world, sound is a sacred tool that can restore your energy and bring peace to your spirit.

As you attune to the vibrations around you, pause to notice what resonates with your heart.

Reflection

- What sounds in your environment lift you up, and which ones drain your energy?
- How do your words and tone influence the energy of those around you?
- How can you intentionally use sound or music to restore harmony in your body and mind?

Affirmation

"My voice, my words, and the sounds I welcome create harmony within me and radiate peace into the world."

"I am attuned to vibrations that uplift, heal, and inspire."

Painful Events

Painful events stand out in our lives. It is not the pain itself but the emotion behind the pain, buried in the creases of our memory, which keeps us stuck in the experience. We may not always remember the details of what happened, but we will always remember how something or someone made us feel. These emotions stay with us until we consciously choose to release them. Letting go is a decision only you can make, and it is the decision that allows you to move forward.

The memory of pain is a powerful one. It alters how you view life, yourself, others, and even God, or whatever term feels true to you when referring to a higher power. You may cry because of the injustice of it all, rage in anger, mourn in sadness, plead in disbelief, or even yell at God before eventually settling down, accepting the event, and weaving it into your life path. This process can take moments, days, or years, depending on the severity of the event and your willingness to let go and accept what has been given to you. Nothing is accidental. Nothing is by chance. Painful events are some of our greatest teachers, guiding us to reflect, release pent-up emotions, forgive the perpetrator, adjust our thinking, and change course.

The greatest changes in our lives often come as a result of pain. If you resist the lesson, you will remain stuck in anger, sadness, or depression. The more you fight your emotions, the more trapped you become. The way forward is to step back, observe the event from the outside rather than from within, and see your emotions with clarity, not from a victim's perspective, but from a higher one. From there, you can decide your next step. The more you accept and allow this process to unfold, the quicker you move through pain into wisdom. You do not return to the "old you," but instead step into a newer, stronger, and wiser version of yourself.

Rather than looking at painful events with dread, it is possible to see them as opportunities for growth and expansion. These are the moments that reveal who you truly are and what you truly want from life. They bring forth your truth, your real self. Therefore, do not fight them. Accept the change, release the emotions, and move forward.

Life is like the ocean with its ebb and flow. Waves are always moving back and forth; some may be rough and high, others calm and soothing, yet in the end they are all part of the whole and return to the ocean. Your challenge is to ride the waves with as much grace as you can, so growth and transformation can take place. Step into the lesson instead of running away, let go of resistance, and allow your Soul to expand.

Reflection

- What painful events in your life still linger in your memory, and what emotions remain attached to them?
- Can you step back and view these experiences as teachers rather than punishments?
- What new version of yourself might be waiting on the other side of release?

Affirmation

"I ride the waves of life with courage and grace."
"Every painful event becomes a steppingstone to my higher self and a doorway to wisdom."

Natural Flow

There is a natural flow to the Universe. When we hold space for this flow to enter our lives, the Universe gives us the green light. Like a beacon, it becomes our rudder, guiding us at every moment. When things move with ease, synchronicity has a chance to enter, showing us that we are on the right track, doing exactly what we are meant to do, and being exactly where you are supposed to be.

The opposite is also true. When things feel hard, resistant, or like a struggle, it may be a sign that we are not in alignment with what we are meant to be doing or where we are meant to be at this point in our lives. Our personal barometer is speaking to us, but so often we choose to ignore it. This barometer is always available within us. It is the quiet inner voice, intuition, which lets us know what direction to pursue. Too often, we feel guided one way, only to have our mind (ego) override it. Sadly, more often than not, we not only dismiss our inner guidance but even go in the opposite direction of what our intuition tells us.

In today's society many people choose to self-medicate with pre-scription drugs, alcohol, or other substances to numb themselves, escape their reality, or quiet the pain they feel inside. This is often because we have lost the ability to trust our own inner wisdom. Instead of moving with the flow, we react to the drama around us instead of consciously acting from a place of inner truth.

Think of those days when nothing seems to go right. The moment you arrive at work, something breaks down, clients are difficult, technology fails, and appointments pile up. By the end of the day, you feel exhausted, depleted, and discouraged. At these times, you want to hide from the world and use any means necessary to escape reality, food, substances, or distractions.

Now, think of the opposite. Imagine you are on your way to work, and every traffic light turns green. You arrive early, your meetings run smoothly, phone calls are pleasant, and the day unfolds with ease. At the end of the day, you feel satisfied, energized, and accomplished. You have plenty of energy left to enjoy your hobbies, your family, and your friends.

These contrasting emotions are part of your inner guidance system. They are always accessible to you, no matter where you are or what is happening around you. When something feels good, warm, exciting, and uplifting, it is aligned with you — so keep moving forward. When something feels wrong, stressful, heavy, draining, or fearful, it is not the right path for you in that moment. Step back, take a deep breath, and redirect yourself. Wait for a better opening by listening to your unique guidance system. Do not ignore it. It will always lead you where you need to go.

By honoring your inner voice, you empower yourself, attract greater energy, and start to merge with the natural flow of the universe. It is a win-win situation, so start listening and walk in the flow of your Soul.

Reflection

- Think of a time when everything flowed easily in your life. How did it feel?
- Recall a time when everything felt heavy or stuck. What was your inner voice telling you that you may have ignored?
- How can you recognize the signs, or feelings, which show when you are in the natural flow of life versus when you are resisting it?

Affirmation

"I trust my inner guidance. I allow life to flow with ease, knowing that when I follow what feels true and light, I am exactly where I am meant to be."

Path of Least Resistance

While incarnated, we often choose the path of least resistance. Many of the choices we make daily, monthly, or even yearly are simply to keep moving forward. Unfortunately, most of us live in a state of denial, under the illusion that everything is fine. We believe that if we don't rock the boat, we'll be okay. Sound familiar?

Some might say, "*Not me, I tell it like it is.*" But are you really? What about at work? Do you always act on your truth, or do you sometimes go along with what others say, your boss, for instance? Often, if we look closely, we see that we give in more than we realize or even admit to ourselves.

For all of us, our words and actions stem from a deeper place, whether in business, community, or family. Instead of asking, "*What is best for me? What do I want? What is my truth?* "We often bury our heads in the sand and follow the expectations of others. Conditioned thinking or fear keeps us from standing on our ground. We give in, go along, and act on the opinions of others.

This is especially true for women. From an early age, many are taught to be nice, to listen, not to get angry, to be "good girls," or, in some cultures, to be seen and not heard. Men are not exempt from this conditioning, but the burden is often heavier for women.

In these changing times, we are all being asked to energetically confront ourselves, our past, our relationships, and the choices we've made. As we do this, it becomes essential to stay calm, grounded, and balanced.

Life inevitably confronts us with the consequences of our choices. It's important to remember that there are no wrong choices or wrong turns, only opportunities and lessons. We are here to expand our souls, and from the soul's perspective, there is no right or wrong, only growth.

The path of least resistance is found when we accept this truth and stop labeling our experiences as failures. When we move with life rather than against it, even difficult moments become part of a natural unfolding that guides us forward.

If there are moments in your life that bring shame or regret, shift how you see them. Each one was a steppingstone, moving you closer to who you are meant to be. Without those lessons, you wouldn't be the person you are today. Ask yourself, *"What did I learn from this choice, situation, or event?"* Then let go and move forward.

The path of least resistance opens when you stop fighting the past and allow its lessons to integrate. Staying stuck in the past serves no one, least of all yourself. Reflection is healthy, but release is necessary.

If you want to sing, sing. If you want to jump out of an airplane, jump. You are the creator of your life. Nobody else walks in your shoes, so why wait for their blessing or approval? Fulfillment comes when you follow your own path, and you have the strength to do so. Everything you need is already within you. Have faith, and the path will unfold.

Reflection

- In what areas of your life do you tend to take the path of least resistance?
- Where do you hold back from speaking your truth out of fear or conditioning?
- What would your life look like if you fully trusted your own guidance and followed it fearlessly?

Affirmation

"I have the courage to walk my own path. I release fear, trust my inner truth, and let my light shine freely."

Being of Service

Helpfulness is a powerful force that shifts your energy. When you turn your attention away from your own struggles and toward being of service, you raise your vibration and uplift the energy of those around you.

The rewards for helpfulness are immense. Offering a hand, a kind word, or support not only lightens another's load but also shifts your own perspective. The cycle of service releases endorphins, creates joy, and sets positive change into motion. The more you help, the more you feel purposeful, connected, and at peace.

To help is to serve, and to serve others is to serve the greater whole. When you place yourself in the hands of Universal Consciousness life gently guides you into situations where your presence and kindness are needed. You may never know why a certain person or circumstance appears in your path, but when you answer the call to be helpful, you align with the divine current of purpose and love.

What once weighed heavily on your heart may suddenly seem less significant. By shifting the focus from your own challenges to the needs of another, you invite light and hope into your life. Helpfulness transforms you; it reminds you that even one small act can ripple outward, touching lives in ways you may never see, yet returning joy to your own heart in the process.

The Universe always matches what you give. The more you share your time, compassion, and love, the more abundance flows back to you. The return may not come as money or recognition but as peace, gratitude, and renewed strength. When you feel low, step outside yourself and see where you can make a difference. Sometimes it's the smallest gesture, a smile, a kind word, a quiet presence. that can change someone's entire day. No act is ever too small. Yes, one person can make a difference—and it begins with you being open to serve.

Reflection

- When was the last time you helped someone without expecting anything in return?
- How does serving others shift your perspective on your own struggles?
- In what small ways can you practice helpfulness today?

Affirmation

"I open my heart to serve with love. Through helping others, I am uplifted, healed, and renewed."

The Expression of Love

There are many ways we express love, through a smile, a gentle touch, or an action offered for the benefit of another. At times it comes naturally, while other times our expression may feel blocked or forced. The expression of love becomes natural when we step out of our own way and allow it to move through us freely. Yet for many of us, love is often filtered through fear. That fear is rarely about the present moment; it is shaped by past pain, unresolved experiences, and emotional wounds we carry with us. To express love fully, we must be willing to meet those old hurts, heal them, and release the energy attached to them.

We all carry residual energy from past events, whether those experiences were caused by others or by choices we made ourselves. Until those emotions are acknowledged and processed, they quietly influence how safe we feel opening our hearts. Healing is not about reliving the past; it is about freeing yourself from it so love no longer feels risky.

Many people still hold the belief that we are only physical beings. Either they cannot see beyond the body, or they resist the idea that we are spiritual beings having a human experience. Yet you are far more than flesh and bone. You are energy, consciousness, and light, formed from love itself. When we disconnect from this truth, we lose touch with our intuition and our deeper sense of well-being, both emotionally and spiritually. And when we lose touch with ourselves, our ability to express love becomes limited, filtered through fear, conditioning, and expectation rather than flowing freely from our true nature. Remembering who you are restores that flow. Love then becomes less about effort and more about expression, a natural extension of the light and awareness that already live within you.

This inner work matters because energy responds to energy. A fearful mindset attracts more fear, while a loving mindset invites connection and ease. Go inward. Clear what no longer feels trust. When you allow love to flow freely, your outer world begins to respond in kind.

To move towards love, try stretching, gently stretching beyond your comfort zone. Express kindness. Offer appreciation. Open your heart, even in small ways, even with strangers. Offer a genuine smile to someone in passing without an agenda, speak kindly to a cashier or server, seeing them more than their role, or offer a simple "thank you" that is felt and not rushed. Most people are longing for the same thing you are, to be seen, acknowledged, and loved. The Universe mirrors what we put out. When you choose love, love finds its way back to you.

Be mindful of your thoughts and words. Express love where you can. It truly is that simple. And in choosing love, again and again, you help create the world you wish to live in.

Reflection

- How easily do I allow love to flow through me without fear or hesitation?
- In what ways has past hurt shaped how I express love?
- What would one day guide fully by love look like for me?
- Who or what can I offer love to today, without expectation of return?

Affirmation

"I am a vessel of divine love."
"I release fear and open my heart to give and receive love freely."
"My essence is light, and through love, I bring warmth and connection into the world."

Spirituality

Spirituality accepts that there is more to life than what we can see with our eyes, that there is a higher power, and that we can view life from a Universal perspective. It is not about religion, nor is it tied to any denomination or philosophy. It is your ability to move beyond immediate circumstances and view life from a wider, more meaningful perspective.

Spirituality allows you to discover your own belief system, giving you the freedom to explore what still resonates and release what no longer serves you. Often, when you begin your spiritual path, you realize that what you were told or raised with may no longer carry meaning. During this time, you may feel isolated, as if you are swimming in an ocean without a life vest. At this crossroad, one of two things can happen:

- You may return to your roots, holding even tighter to your old beliefs, or
- You may feel like a child in a candy store, eager to explore, touch, and see everything that lies ahead.

I have witnessed both paths in friends and acquaintances, those who chose the first often remain stuck, while those who chose the second move forward with greater awareness and freedom. For myself, once I began my spiritual journey, it became a long road of self-discovery, letting go, reinventing myself, and reshaping my views. I do not regret this path, though I recognize I am no longer the person I once was. What I know now, and how I choose to live, is entirely different from where I began.

Oprah's Winfrey's words, "*When you know better, you do better,*" guide me to this day. I am far from perfect, and I stumble just like anyone else. I am human after all. But most of the time, I consciously choose to act from a higher perspective. This is not always easy, especially in the presence of others, but I hold the intention to protect my energy while still making a difference in the world. Over time, I have learned to open myself when I choose to and to close off when protection is needed. Spirituality, as I understand it, is the practice of leading from a higher perspective, rising above momentary challenges to stay connected to what truly matters.

The path of spirituality broadens your horizons, shifts your boundaries, dismantles old beliefs, and opens up an entirely new world. You are not alone. Spiritual beings, crossed-over loved ones, and other forms of higher consciousness surround you at all times. Just because you cannot see, hear, or sense them does not mean they are absent. Trust that they are there, and that they are here to assist you.

How can you believe in something you cannot see? How do you prove love exists? How do you prove faith exists? You cannot touch, see, or measure either, yet both are undeniably real. The same is true of the unseen presence that surrounds you.

Open yourself to new insight, fresh understanding, and different ways of seeing the world. When you are willing to shift perspective, life expands in ways you may not have imagined.

Remember, you are a spiritual being having a human experience, not the other way around. When you lead from that awareness, you rise above the surface details of daily life and begin to respond with clarity rather than habit. Be willing to take a courageous step beyond what feels familiar. When you do, life meets you there. New possibilities emerge, understanding deepens, and a wider world quietly opens before you.

Reflection

- What old beliefs no longer serve you?
- In what ways can you allow yourself to be more open to unseen guidance and support?
- How do you protect your energy while remaining open-hearted?

Affirmation

"I honor myself as a spiritual being having a physical experience. I welcome growth, guidance, and wisdom, trusting that I am never alone on my path."

Pauses for the Soul

Pauses for the Soul are small breathing moments in time, invitations to reflect on our lives. Without them, we simply move from one thing to the next, connecting dots mindlessly until something forces us to stop and ask: *"What happened? Where am I? Where am I going?"*

These pauses don't need to be long. They can be as brief or as spacious as we choose. The key is to take them. Without moments of reflection, we risk finding ourselves on a path we do not like, surrounded by thoughts, emotions, and choices that no longer serve our well-being.

When we repeatedly ignore our inner checkpoints, our sense of well-being begins to decline. What starts as subtle signals, fatigue, emotional disconnection, persistent stress, or a quiet sense of unease, can gradually deepen if left unaddressed. Over time, life brings moments that interrupt our forward momentum and invite us to pause.

These interruptions may appear as a health scare, the loss of a loved one, a major life transition, or an unexpected event that forces us to slow down and reflect. They are not punishments. They are invitations.

Each pause offers an opportunity to gather yourself, tend to your emotional and physical needs, and reassess the direction you are moving in. When met with awareness rather than resistance, these moments become powerful turning points, allowing you to realign, restore balance, and move forward with greater clarity and intention.

Ask yourself: *"Do I like this? Does this work for me? Am I on the right path? Do I need to make adjustments? Where do I want to go next?"* If your answers point toward change, honor them.

Like the sun shining after a storm, these moments always pass. We are never stuck. Freedom will allows us to shift direction at any time.

Yet our ego often resists. We dig in, throw tantrums, and prolong the very discomfort which is meant to guide us forward. When we navigate these periods wisely, flowing instead of fighting, the Universe responds in kind. Things resolve more smoothly, more quickly, and with greater ease.

Taking Soul Pauses is essential to your well-being. Work them gently into your life. The more often you pause, the clearer and freer your perspective becomes. From that clarity, better choices naturally emerge.

Breathe. Pause. Listen. You'll be amazed at what is waiting for you.

Reflection

- When was the last time you gave yourself a true pause to reflect?
- What messages has your Soul been trying to send you that you may have ignored?
- How can you weave short pauses into your daily rhythm starting today?

Affirmation

"I welcome Soul Pauses into my life. Each pause renews my energy, clears my perspective, and guides me back into alignment with my true path."

Self-Love

Self-love is one of the most challenging lessons to learn while living in a physical body. Yet it is absolutely possible. The difficulty does not lie in loving ourselves, but in unlearning what we were taught to believe about who we are.

We arrive in this world pure, open, and free from judgment. As children, we do not question our worth. But as soon as we begin interacting with parents, family, culture, and society, we start absorbing their beliefs, expectations, and limitations. Over time, this conditioning quietly becomes our inner truth. We are told what is right and wrong, what is acceptable and what is not, how to behave, speak, and feel. Before we know it, we are no longer living from our own essence, but through someone else's lens.

Each of us views the world through a personal filter shaped by upbringing, culture, and experience. Two people can read the same page and walk away with completely different interpretations. That same filter influences how we see ourselves. When the filter is distorted by criticism, comparison, or rejection, self-love becomes harder to access.

Many of us try to fill that emptiness by looking outward. We seek love from partners, friends, or approval from others, hoping it will make us feel whole. But no one can give you what you are unwilling to give yourself. External love can support you, but it cannot replace self-love. When you rely on others to fill that space, disappointment often follows. True wholeness begins within. Only you can offer yourself the love you are seeking. And the sooner you begin, the lighter and freer life becomes.

Countless people move through life on autopilot, unaware of how deeply conditioned their responses are. They believe they are authentic, when in fact they are repeating learned patterns. It takes courage to stop and ask:

Who am I?

What do I truly believe?

Is this where I want to be?

Because we all come from different backgrounds and life experiences, our reactions and beliefs naturally differ. No two people move through the world in the same way. When conflict or discomfort arises, it is easy to react from habit or emotion rather than awareness.

This is an invitation to pause.

By slowing down and turning inward, you create space between what happens and how you respond. In that space, you can reconnect with your center and choose to respond from love rather than fear. It is here that self-love takes root, and where healing quietly begins.

When you feel triggered, unsettled, or emotionally charged:

- Pause; resist the urge to respond immediately.
- Breathe; take one slow, intentional breath in through your nose, and exhale fully.
- Turn inward; bring your attention to your body. Notice where you feel tension or emotion without trying to fix it.
- Find your center; place a hand over your heart or lower abdomen and reconnect with your inner steadiness.
- Choose your response; Ask yourself, "*What would love choose here?*" Let your response arise from clarity rather than fear.

This practice does not require perfection. Each pause strengthens your ability to meet yourself, and others, with greater compassion and awareness.

To love yourself fully, you must be willing to meet these questions honestly. Rewriting your inner dialogue takes time, patience, and gentleness. Your mind may resist and slip back into familiar patterns, but with awareness and consistency, a new way of relating to yourself will form.

Begin each day by looking into your own eyes in the mirror. Smile and say, *"Good morning. I love you."* Speak to yourself with kindness. Replace criticism with compassion. Remind yourself that you are worthy, beautiful, and enough. You were created from the same essence as all of creation, how could anything about you be wrong?

Over time, as loving thoughts replace old beliefs, self-love becomes natural rather than forced. You no longer need to remind yourself to love, you simply do. And when that happens, something shifts. You move through life with confidence, openness, and freedom.

So, allow yourself to love who you are, fully and without apology. There is no one better suited for the task than you.

Reflection

- When do I feel most disconnected from self-love?
- How has my upbringing shaped my beliefs about my worth?
- When was the last time I spoke kindly to myself?
- What does unconditional self-love look like for me?
- What is one loving act I can offer myself today?

Affirmation

"I am worthy of my own love."
"I release old conditioning and embrace myself with compassion and grace."
"I am whole, radiant, and enough exactly as I am."

Belief

Belief often begins with what we can perceive through our senses. We tend to trust what we see, touch, hear, smell, or experience directly. In this way, belief feels concrete and verifiable.

Yet belief can also extend beyond what is immediately visible. It includes trusting insights, inner nudges, and experiences that cannot always be measured or proven. Not everything meaningful can be held in your hands or explained through logic alone. Expanding your belief in this way requires courage, particularly when it challenges long-held patterns of thinking.

If you remain anchored solely in your existing belief system, your perception of life remains confined by it. Beliefs act as filters, shaping how you interpret events, relationships, and even yourself.

When you allow those filters to widen, your perspective expands. You become more receptive to new understanding and experiences that may not fit neatly within reason alone. These may arise as sudden clarity, subtle impressions, sensations, or intuitive awareness.

How do you know whether what you perceive is true? For certain experiences, tangible proof may not exist. You may not be able to demonstrate them or offer evidence that satisfies everyone. In those moments, belief becomes a personal choice. You either trust the meaning of what you have experienced, or you do not.

Your body will guide you in the process of believing. It has a built-in alert system that is always available and will never fail you.

When you believe something, your body will give you clues as to whether it is true for you or not. Even if your mind doubts it, this system always tells the truth. When you believe in something, your body feels open, warm, and acceptable. When you do not, your body protects itself and closes off, sometimes creating tension, resistance, or discomfort. Once you start recognizing your body's signals and accept them as your truth, your personal guidance, you can move forward in life with greater ease and trust.

Trust your body; it will always tell you the truth, your truth. When you question your belief in something, go within and listen. Begin to rely on this inner compass. Belief is not tangible, yet your body can always distinguish what supports you and what does not. Your body does not lie. Trust your gut, trust what you are seeing, and keep going.

Belief is yours and yours alone. Nobody can take it away or alter it. Stay strong in your belief and in your life. Venture into the unknown bravely and with trust, for you have the tools to guide you along the way. The path to empowerment begins with knowing that something better is waiting for you. That in itself is a belief. So, jump in, don't hold back, and live your best life.

Reflection

- What does believe mean to me personally, beyond religious context?
- How does my body guide me in knowing what I truly believe?
- Where might I be holding back from trusting the unseen?

Affirmation

"I trust the Universe to guide me. I open my heart to miracles, big and small. I honor my inner guidance and follow my beliefs with courage and faith. I am aligned with the path meant for me."

Honor

To live with honor is to hold ourselves to a higher standing of being, to pursue what benefits not only ourselves, but the greater community. Honor is doing what is right even when no one is watching. Honor is a character trait we choose to live by. We either value it and embody it, or we do not. To live with honor is to hold yourself to a higher standard of integrity, choosing actions that benefit not only yourself but also those around you. It shows itself in everyday moments, keeping your word when it would be easier to break it, speaking truthfully even when it is uncomfortable, and acting with fairness when no one is watching.

In many communities, the act of honoring others is expressed outwardly, such as by bowing when meeting or parting. This simple gesture allows the one receiving it to feel acknowledged, respected, and seen. To honor this small gesture and curtesy honor those that you encounter. At the core, is this not what we all seek, recognition, validation, and the feeling of being valued? Honor enables us to hold our heads high and stand in our full presence while allowing others to do the same. Honor means we live free from the weight of guilt or shame.

When we honor others, whether by listening with full presence, showing genuine respect, or acknowledging their inherent worth, we uplift them. To honor someone is to communicate, *"I see you. You matter."* In doing so, we create space for them to stand more confidently in who they are.

Honor does not always require words. It is revealed in how you carry yourself, in the attentiveness behind your gestures, and in the consistency of how you treat those around you. It is expressed through integrity, fairness, and quiet recognition. What is often overlooked is that honor is reciprocal. When you extend it freely, you strengthen your own character and invite the same respect in return.

The ability to honor others begins with honoring yourself. If you do not live with honor within, it is difficult to extend it outward. Actions that arise from honor come from a higher place of existence. From the mindset of honor, you do not lie, you do not steal, you do not harm. Instead, you move with consciousness and kindness. You practice self-care regularly and give yourself the gift of self-reflection. You step back, breathe and plan your next course of action with patience and thoughtfulness. Honor is a two-way street: give honor and people respect you, think with honor and it is reflected back to you. Actions that arise from honor come from a higher place of existence.

By living in a state of honor, you make the world a better place. Your energy naturally spreads to everyone and everything you encounter. People, animals, and even the environment sense your reliability and integrity. What a gift it is to the world to know that simply by being yourself, walking tall in your honor, you bring light and positive impact into the lives of others.

So go out, walk in confidence, in honor of yourself, of others, and of humankind.

Reflection
- How do I honor myself in my daily life?
- In what ways can I show honor to others through my actions and energy?
- Where in my life can I hold myself to a higher standard and give honor to myself and others?

Excitement

Excitement is the energy of renewal, hope, and fresh beginnings. It feeds our soul, sparks curiosity, and fills us with wonder about what life may bring next. Just as a child delights in exploring a new toy, excitement invites us to explore new possibilities in our surroundings, and more importantly, within ourselves.

As a teenager stepping into adulthood, we experience this firsthand. Graduation ushers us into the real world, where choices about work, school, and career begin to take shape. While this transition can feel overwhelming, it is often accompanied by a deep sense of excitement for the possibilities ahead. That same energy appears at other turning points in life, the beginning of a new relationship, moving to another country, or discovering a new hobby that sparks curiosity and joy. These moments fill you with hope, vitality, and the anticipation of becoming something more.

As adults, daily routines and responsibilities often keep us within the safety of the familiar, a space that stands in clear contrast to excitement, growth, and expansion. When life becomes too predictable, energy can stagnate and the spirit begins to dull. New energy, however, has the opposite effect. It awakens curiosity, inspires fresh thinking, and opens the door to new opportunities, connections, and insights.

While we may not always be able to change our commitments or responsibilities, we can change the way we experience them. A shift in perspective can bring new life to even the most familiar routines. Something as simple as taking a different route to work, trying a new activity, learning a new skill, or engaging in conversations with people who see the world differently can introduce fresh energy into your life. Reading a book outside your usual interests, spending time in nature, or setting aside quiet moments for reflection can also invite new ideas and inspiration.

By gently stepping beyond the familiar, even in small ways, you create space for renewed perspective and possibility. Growth does not always require dramatic change. Often it begins with curiosity and a willingness to see the world, and yourself, with fresh eyes.

Embracing change is essential. Excitement grows from trusting that the unknown holds something valuable for you. Change is not something to fear, it is the path to growth. If you feel stuck or your energy has grown dull, invite something new into your life, even in the smallest way, and allow the excitement of possibility to awaken the part of you that is ready to grow.

Have faith, take the leap, and let excitement carry you forward.

Reflection
- What areas of my life feel stagnant or dull right now?
- Where can I invite more excitement by shifting my perspective?
- What opportunities might be waiting for me if I let go of fear and embrace change?

Affirmation
"I welcome excitement into my life."
"I embrace change with courage, curiosity, and joy, knowing the Universe is guiding me toward my highest purpose."

Miracles

M iracles surround us everywhere we look. From the leaves growing on trees, a smile on someone's face or the sudden lift in
spirit when something new awakens our curiosity, miracles exist in
the smallest details, quietly making a difference every time. Miracles
are not magic; they are the little things that stand out and positively
influence the world around us. Take the sun, for instance. Just by
rising every morning, it gives life. Everything the sun touches grows,
creating nourishment and allowing life to flourish.

Your life is filled with miracles, and although many may not
always see them, they are found in the small details and choices
that align with the Universe. Random acts of kindness, people who
suddenly enter your life, or visions that come to pass are all small
miracles. When you align with the vibration of the Universe, more
of the same can enter your life. By focusing on your blessings rather
than your shortcomings, you show the Universe that you are ready
and willing to receive more, inviting abundance and flow into your
experience.

During this process, your ego may become a hurdle you must
face and overcome. The ego is always active, questioning everything
it encounters. It does not like change; it prefers things just the way
they are. It is said that it takes about 21 days to change a habit or
behavior, mainly because your ego holds on tightly and resists the
shift. The ego survives within the set parameters of the moment;

however, in time, as your thoughts shift, so will those parameters, and by default, the ego's defenses will shift as well. Ironically, it will then protect the boundaries of the new parameters with the same determination. So don't be fooled by the intensity of resistance, it is, in its own way, an illusion.

To overcome this hurdle, do not fight it. Let it move through you and then let it pass. The more effort you put into resisting, the harder your journey will become, and the more difficult it will be for miracles to enter your world. Be patient with yourself and focus on the positive. Don't expect miracles, take each day as it comes. The more you free your mind, the more you can allow miracles, both big and small, to enter your life. Pay attention to the smallest details, and you will find perfection in each one. The Universe does not make mistakes, so enjoy what is already here and allow life to unfold. Miracles are everywhere when you know where, and how, to look.

Reflection

- What miracles, big or small, have shown up in your life this week?
- How would your perspective shift if you began to actively look for them each day?

Affirmation

"I open my heart and eyes to the miracles around me. I trust that the Universe is always guiding me with love, abundance, and divine timing."

Desire

Desire is the emotion of wanting to achieve or obtain something. An object of desire can be a thing, a place, a person, or even a spiritual state of mind. What we do with that desire is entirely in our hands.

We have all heard the expression, *"The road to hell is paved with good intentions."* Desire alone doesn't move us forward without action behind it. For example, if we want to lose weight but don't change our eating habits or begin to exercise, the desire will remain a wish without results. To achieve a desire, we must do the work and change our habits so the outcome can manifest.

On a spiritual level, desire can be a helpful emotion, yet it can also feel defeating. On a spiritual level, desire can be a helpful emotion, yet it can also feel defeating. Desire can motivate us to grow, to pursue new opportunities, or to follow a calling that brings deeper meaning to our lives. At the same time, when desire turns into attachment or expectation, it can create frustration and disappointment when things do not unfold the way we hoped. For example, the desire to build a meaningful career can inspire dedication and perseverance, yet if we measure our worth solely by success or recognition, that same desire can leave us feeling discouraged or unfulfilled.

Desire requires more than simply wanting something, it calls for alignment between thought, emotion, and action. Consider the example of wanting to build a meaningful career. Your thoughts begin with clarity about what inspires you and the belief that your efforts can lead somewhere purposeful. Emotionally, you cultivate enthusiasm and openness toward the possibilities ahead rather than focusing on doubt or frustration about what has not yet happened. From there, action naturally follows through practical steps such as learning new skills, seeking opportunities, connecting with mentors, or dedicating time each day to move closer to your goal.

The Law of Attraction reminds us that the Universe reflects back the energy we send out. When we focus on doubt, worry, or negativity, those emotions tend to echo back into our experience. When we focus on trust, openness, and possibility, those energies return to us as well. So, if we desire something meaningful, perhaps a fulfilling career, a loving relationship, or a deeper sense of purpose, and we take steps toward it while quietly thinking, "*This will probably never work,*" or "*I'm not good enough,*" our inner resistance can block the very outcome we hope for. However, when we intentionally shift our inner dialogue and remind ourselves, through affirmations or quiet mantras, that "*I am capable,*" "*Opportunities are unfolding for me,*" or "*I trust the path ahead,*" our thoughts, emotions, and actions begin to align.

In many ways, the Universe responds to the tone we set within ourselves. Like attracts like. When our inner world and outer actions move in the same direction, the path forward becomes clearer, and the puzzle pieces begin to fall into place.

Desires manifest when your thoughts, emotions, and vibration all match. In that moment, a doorway opens for new experiences and opportunities to enter your life. To do this, raise your vibration in both your physical and emotional bodies. Focus your energy toward your goals, while releasing what keeps you stuck in your current state of mind. Establish your desires, raise your frequency, and create space for your desires to find you.

Reflection

- What desire has been sitting in my heart for a long time?
- What actions or habits are needed to bring it closer?
- Where might I need to release fear, doubt, or old patterns to align myself with it?

Affirmation

*"I raise my vibration, align my thoughts and actions, and open the
doorway for my desires to manifest."*

Equilibrium

Life carries within it a silver thread. This thread is called equilibrium. By definition, equilibrium is a delicate balance between two polar opposites. Too much of anything can upset this balance, shifting the natural flow out of harmony, leaving you feeling off, unwell, or even emotionally heavy.

Life carries within it a silver thread. This thread is called equilibrium. By definition, equilibrium is a delicate balance between two polar opposites. Too much of anything can upset this balance, shifting the natural flow out of harmony, leaving you feeling off, unwell, or even emotionally heavy.

A beautiful example of this can be seen in Yellowstone National Park. For years, the park's ecosystem was out of balance, leaning too far to one side. The deer population had grown too large, leading to overgrazing and loss of habitat. With the reintroduction of just fourteen wolves, the balance slowly began to restore itself. The deer population came under control, which allowed new trees, bushes, and grasses to grow again. These plants provided shelter for birds and small rodents, which in turn attracted hawks and eagles, creating balance across the food chain. What was once considered a dangerous animal became respected for its vital role in the natural order. Wolves, once hunted nearly to extinction, now thrive through conservation and reintroduction programs worldwide, restoring balance where it was once lost.

The same principle of equilibrium applies to us. When we consume too much of anything, whether food, information, or energy, our bodies and minds shift out of balance. This can leave us feeling heavy, cluttered, and disconnected. By reducing excess and allowing moderation in all areas of life, our body and spirit naturally return to their harmonious state.

This applies to your environment as well. When we accumulate too many things, our homes can begin to feel cluttered and overwhelming, and the energy around us may start to feel stagnant. Yet with intention and care, we can restore our space, so it once again feels peaceful, safe, and supportive. Begin with small, manageable steps, clearing one surface or drawer at a time and letting go of items that no longer serve a purpose. You can also invite fresh energy into your home by opening the windows, allowing natural light and air to circulate, or by rearranging a space so it feels more open and balanced. These simple actions create room for calm, clarity, and renewed energy to enter.

Balance begins within the body. Care for it through simple, restorative practices such as gentle movement, mindful breathing, or moments of quiet rest. When your body is balanced, you will notice a sense of ease, steadiness, and renewed energy.

Balance your spirit as well. Use the reflections and affirmations in this chapter and throughout the book to reconnect with yourself. Spend time in nature, allow your thoughts to settle, and return to the quiet place within where clarity and guidance can be heard.

Balance your environment. At the beginning of each season, take time to refresh your surroundings. Clear away what has accumulated, organize what remains, and let go of items that no longer serve you. By creating space in your physical environment, you invite new energy and fresh possibilities into your life.

When equilibrium is restored, energy begins to move freely again. Life starts to feel lighter and more aligned. Doors that once seemed closed may quietly open, and new opportunities appear where there was once resistance. Find your equilibrium and allow yourself the freedom to live the life you envision.

Reflection

- Where in your life are things out of balance, your body, your emotions, your environment, or your relationships?
- What is one small step you can take today to restore balance and create more flow?

Affirmation

"I restore balance in my body, mind, and environment."
"I invite harmony, flow, and renewal into my life."

Gratitude

The fastest way to change our energy is by being grateful. Gratitude shifts our perspective from negative to positive. When we focus on the good things in your life and let go of the past, your energy begins to shift, and a new perspective can become our new reality.

Replacing a negative thought instantly changes the course of your life for the brain cannot hold on to a negative thought when a positive one comes into play, like opening a window in a stuffy room, allowing fresh air to move through and clear the space."

When I started to type the words on this page, I accidentally misspelled the word *gratefulness* and wrote *great-fullness*. What an inspiring truth: when we are grateful, we are filled with greatness. Gratitude places us in a space of fullness, where we feel whole and alive.

When we are thankful, we recognize all the actions we have taken to get us where we are today. Gratitude allows us to notice and see the smaller details that we often overlook due to busy schedules or distracted thinking. Even the difficult choices and challenging moments have shown us how resilient and determined we are, leaving us feeling empowered and maybe even curious about what comes next.

Get into the habit of being grateful for everything you encounter. Remember that even the smallest events can shape our day, week, or month. Try to see the beauty in every experience placed before us, because there are always lessons to be learned. The next time you are standing in line at the grocery store, instead of focusing on the wait, take a moment to notice something simple, the kindness of a cashier helping someone, the abundance of food around you, or the opportunity to slow down for a moment in a busy day. Or when you step outside in the morning, pause for a moment and appreciate the fresh air, the warmth of the sun, or the quiet stillness before the day begins. Even in frustrating moments, such as being stuck in traffic, you can shift your perspective. Instead of reacting with anger, use the time to breathe, listen to music or a podcast you enjoy, or simply appreciate the pause before the next part of your day begins.

Start each day with a fresh and open mind and write down a few things you are grateful for. Gratitude can be as simple as being thankful for waking up, enjoying your morning coffee, or appreciating the love of your friends and family.

Gratefulness equals feeling great. It opens doors and allows you to see everything in a new light, attracting new opportunities. Gratefulness gives you the mindset and energy to change course, it is the path to enlightenment. When you love your life, you naturally love yourself, and in that space, you are able to love others more freely. Loving others allows your warm energy to flow outward, inviting harmony and change into your world.

You can change your life simply by starting each day with gratitude. Check in with yourself at lunchtime or dinner and reflect on your day. Find the moments that brought you peace, gratitude, or a quiet lesson. You'll be amazed by the transformation you'll see in a very short time. Be consistent, and you'll feel the difference, not just in your thoughts, but in the way you move through life. When you feel great, you become confident, capable, and grounded. It's so simple, yet so powerful, and it can truly change your life for the better.

Reflection

Take a moment to reflect on your day and notice the moments that brought you gratitude.

- What small moments today made you pause, smile, or feel at ease?
- Did a challenge reveal a lesson or strength you had not noticed before?
- How did gratitude shift your mood, your perspective, or your energy?

Consider writing down three simple things you are grateful for today, even if they seem small.

Affirmation

"I choose gratitude in every moment."
"With appreciation, I transform my thoughts, my energy, and the direction of my life."
"The more I give thanks, the more life gives back."

Final Thoughts

Change is rarely easy, yet it is essential. Without change there can be no growth, and without growth there is no expansion. Each step you take toward greater awareness, honesty, and courage opens the door to a fuller version of yourself.

Ask yourself what life could become if you allow that change to unfold. The light within you was never meant to stay hidden. Choose growth, happiness, and the path that calls you forward, even when it feels unfamiliar.

No one else can walk that path for you, but no one can stop you from becoming the person you are meant to be either. The only thing required is your willingness to begin.

Take the first step.

In love and gratitude,

Lara